TECHNOLOGY, EDUCATION—CONNECTIONS
THE TEC SERIES

Series Editor: Marcia C. Linn
Advisory Board: Robert Bjork, Chris Dede, Joseph Krajcik, Carol Lee,
Jim Minstrell, Jonathan Osborne, Mitch Resnick, Constance Steinkuehler

Rethinking Education in the Age of Technology

The Digital Revolution and Schooling in America

SECOND EDITION

Allan Collins
Richard Halverson

Foreword by James Paul Gee

TEACHERS COLLEGE PRESS

TEACHERS COLLEGE | COLUMBIA UNIVERSITY
NEW YORK AND LONDON

Published by Teachers College Press, 1234 Amsterdam Avenue, New York, NY 10027

Library of Congress Cataloging-in-Publication Data

Names: Collins, Allan, 1937– | Halverson, Richard author.
Title: Rethinking education in the age of technology : the digital revolution and
    schooling in America / Allan Collins, Richard Halverson; foreword by James
    Paul Gee.
Other titles: Digital revolution and schooling in America
Description: Second edition. | New York : Teachers College Press, Columbia
    University, [2018] | Series: Technology, Education—Connections (The TEC
    Series) | Previous edition: 2009. | Includes bibliographical references and
    index.
Identifiers: LCCN 2017060004(print) | LCCN 2018005561 (ebook) | ISBN
    9780807776919 (ebook) | ISBN 9780807759066 (paperback : acid-free paper)
Subjects: LCSH: Education—Effect of technological innovations on—United
    States. | Educational technology—United States. | Educational change—United
    States. | Technological innovations—Social aspects—United States.
Classification: LCC LB1028.3 (ebook) | LCC LB1028.3 .C636 2018 (print) | DDC
    371.330973—dc23
LC record available at https://lccn.loc.gov/2017060004

ISBN 978-0-8077-5906-6 (paper)
ISBN 978-0-8077-7691-9 (ebook)

Printed on acid-free paper
Manufactured in the United States of America

25 24 23 22 21 20 19 18   8 7 6 5 4 3 2 1

Contents

Foreword

The ancient Greeks and Romans invented a marvelous way to memorize things when knowledge was stored in heads rather than books. The method has been called "the memory palace," "the journey method," or, less memorably, "the method of *loci*." Using this method, a person imagines some well-known building or landscape. Then the person walks in a certain order through different locations within the building or landscape, deposits an item to be recalled in each location, and forms a vivid image of the item in that place. Eventually, after some practice, the person can recall the items by walking around the locations in the memory palace that they have created and retrieving each one. Each item is made highly recallable because of its vivid, imagistic association with a well-known location that is part of a larger connected whole. Aristotle called the locations (*loci*) in memory palaces *topoi*, thereby giving us the English word *topic*. Memory places were invented at a time when memory—not just texts—was crucial to teaching and learning.

After the invention of printing, memory ceased to be the key to learning and learning ceased to be a journey across places in palaces. Instead, knowledge was deposited in books and transmitted in schoolrooms. The invention of school is among humanity's greatest and most successful inventions. It has outpaced the old Greeks and Romans in making education more equitable and accessible, while nonetheless severing the ancient tie of learning to imagery and journeys. Just as the Greeks and Romans added memorial content to places, they powerfully added myth and stories (some epic) to give deep ancestral and historical meaning to everyday people, places, and events. This, too, was lost.

Today, however, young people regularly go on magical journeys in modern "memory palaces." The *loci* now are physical, virtual, and imaginary locations. Here is one such modern journey:

A 15-year-old girl wants to write graphic fan fiction, but as of now, she is a poor writer. She has been inspired by entering the magical world of *The Sims*, a family and community simulator that is the best-selling video game in history. She wants to create stories by modifying images from *The Sims*, adding words to them, and then sequencing them into a story. She goes on a journey. She moves across—back and forth—a set of connected spaces, some real and some virtual.

She moves from *The Sims* virtual world to *Sims* interest-driven Internet sites dealing with all aspects of the game, where fellow fans lead her to *Sims* graphic fan-fiction sites, where, in turn, she is guided to genre writing sites and Photoshopping sites. She frequents various other sites as well, where more advanced writers post their stories. Eventually, she posts some of her own, getting lots of feedback and help. Eventually, she creates her own website and learns how to manage her ever-growing fan base. Her home, her friends' homes, *Sims* conventions, and the larger real and virtual places where vampire romance fan fiction is read and discussed all become part of a real-virtual meld of spaces constituting an infinite number of possible journeys. Today, the girl has thousands of devoted readers.

On her journey, the girl has learned how to "mod" (modify) game software; to use game design and Adobe Photoshop tools; to create and maintain a highly trafficked personal website; to link her website and stories to other *Sims* fan sites to create a network; to make custom characters, events, and environments; to access and design tutorials for various skills as needed; to write a compelling narrative; to match eye-catching images with text; to recruit readers (i.e., advertise her stories, use banners as advertisements, create "teasers," etc.); to edit and stage her story images (using such techniques as shading and cropping); to post text and images on her website to attract new readers and motivate old ones; to respond to fans, especially emotionally in ways that help them; to connect them to a community (which requires a very different kind of language than she uses in her stories); and to work with volunteer editors from her fan base to meet prevailing community standards.

The girl did not journey through a "palace," where she put items in specific rooms. She journeyed through a connected set of real and virtual spaces, inside which she and many others made and placed teaching and learning practices and tools of all different sorts. This is to say, they distributed teaching and learning across many people, tools, and practices. Sometimes the girl learned, sometimes she taught; sometimes she led, sometimes she followed; sometimes she designed, sometimes she used others' designs. Some practices and tools were didactic; some were coaching, modeling, and mentoring; some were discussion, participation, and collaboration; some were textual, others multimodal; some were even tests.

I have characterized such teaching and learning as journeys through "affinity spaces" (connected spaces where people with a shared interest or passion journey to learn and grow), which I also call "distributed teaching and learning spaces." Today, people, if they have access, help, and mentoring, can use such journeys to learn—and master if they wish—almost anything: game design or media production, citizen science or journalism, social activism of all different sorts, robotics, mythology and the history of ancient civilizations, and many other subjects. I myself used just such a journey to learn how to raise chickens and keep them safe (they are doing fine, thanks).

Such journeys are the product of emergent bottom-up and top-down, ever-evolving creation. Like all new inventions, they can be powerful, for good or ill. Just as the 15-year-old girl learned valuable 21st-century skills by moving through affinity space, so, too, do people who want to learn how to be terrorists or hide their ill-gotten gains from government and taxes (the affinity spaces devoted to such efforts are often on the so-called Dark Web). If we want good for our children, we educators must step up to the plate as adults and mentor, guide, design, aggregate, and curate them in the name of the good that we advocate.

Allan Collins and Richard Halverson, in the second edition of their already highly impactful book, are pointing to the powerful out-of-school teaching and learning journeys that kids can take today. They are not by any means arguing that teachers or schools should go away. Rather, they are saying that they should open their doors and windows, connect to other real and virtual places, be crucial tour guides, and send their children on flights of fancy through our modern memory palaces. Of course, we don't fully know yet how to do this. That's the exciting bit, and where this book becomes a preface to new and crucial journeys for us as educators.

—James Paul Gee, Mary Lou Fulton Presidential Professor of Literacy Studies, Regents' Professor, Arizona State University

Acknowledgments

We developed the ideas for this book when we taught a course together on the history of education reform at Northwestern University. Allan continued to teach the course, and Rich adapted many of the ideas that we discussed for his courses at the University of Wisconsin–Madison. We thank all the students and colleagues in the course over the years for their comments on previous drafts of the book. In particular, we would like to thank Le Zhong, for a suggestion about how to improve Chapter 5, which we incorporated into later drafts of the book; Erica R. Halverson, for her insightful comments on the initial drafts; and Julie Kallio and Sarah Hackett for their suggestions on the second-edition revisions. Carol Kountz helped us decide what material to keep in the book and what material to delete. Shirley Brice Heath's comments on an earlier draft and suggestions for revision were invaluable. We also want to thank Donald A. Norman for his encouragement and suggestions for how to write the book to appeal to a general audience; and to the anonymous reviewers, for their suggestions that led to extensive revisions to the manuscript.

Our series editor, Marcia Linn, was critical to bringing us to Teachers College Press, and our editors there, Meg Lemke and Emily Spangler, worked very hard to make the manuscript presentable for teachers and a general audience. We thank James Paul Gee for writing a Foreword to this second edition. John Seely Brown was kind enough to write a Foreword for the first edition of the book, for which we are also grateful. Finally, we want to thank David Williamson Shaffer for his suggestions on how to publicize the book, and Larry Erlbaum, David Perkins, Roy Pea, and Barbara Means for their help in finding a publisher.

Preface to the First Edition

> I have not even intended to judge whether this social revolution, which I believe to be irresistible, is advantageous or disastrous for mankind. I have acknowledged that this revolution is already accomplished or about to be so and I have chosen among those people who have experienced its effects the one in which its development has been the most comprehensive and peaceful, in order that I may make out clearly its natural consequences and the means of turning it to men's advantage. I confess that in America I have seen more than America itself; I have looked there for an image of the essence of democracy, its limitations, its personality, its prejudices, its passions; my wish has been to know it if only to realize at least what we have to fear or hope from it. (de Tocqueville, 2003, pp. 23–24)

Like de Tocqueville, we set out to describe an American revolution. It is the second educational revolution to occur in America, following almost 200 years after the revolution that took us from apprenticeship to universal schooling. New media technologies challenge schooling as the main place where learning occurs. The revolution is by no means a finished work, just as democracy in America was not a finished work in 1831 when de Tocqueville visited America. Again, like de Tocqueville, we try to look at this revolution with all its challenges and its promise. The revolution is advancing globally, but America appears to be at the leading edge, just as it was in the democracy revolution.

Who will benefit, ultimately, in the aftermath of this revolution? In America there is a commercial push to sell educational products to consumers who are looking for an edge up in the race for success. This means that technological products and services are popping up all over the American landscape. Education, once viewed as a public good with equal access for all, is now up for sale to those who can afford specialized services and computer programs.

The trouble with being in the vanguard of such a revolution is the problem it causes for people unable or unwilling to cope with the changes. As American education shifts, new inequities creep into the system. Because of widening disparities in income, we are seeing technological advantages given to the wealthy that exacerbate their social and cultural advantages that were already so apparent. The wealthy have a disproportionate voice in the development of new learning pathways, and take disproportionate advantage of the new learning resources. In the middle of all these changes, our educational landscape is becoming more varied, richer, and more confusing than before.

In our careers, we are seen as advocates for advancing the use of technology in learning, but this book is about how we see the very definition and experience of education radically changing under the pressure of explosive developments in information technologies. We recognize our biases from working as foot soldiers in the transformation of education in America, but we try to step back from them in this book, to take a big picture view.

We think schools have served America and the world very well. When reviewed 500 years from now, the emergence of universal public schooling might well become the signature achievement of the 20th century. We greatly admire the teachers who have dedicated themselves to helping children from different backgrounds to learn and thrive in a changing world, and the leaders who continuously adapt existing school structures and resources to the needs of new families and community. Schools make invaluable contributions to the world's development and we think they will continue to do so well into the future. Our role here is not to vilify schools or public education, but instead to show how the terrain is changing the everyday practices of teaching and learning right under the feet of professional educators.

We argue that the key linkage made over the past century has been the equation of education with schooling. We think it is time that educators and policy makers start to rethink this equation. Education is now a lifelong enterprise, while schooling for most people encompasses only the years between ages 5 and 18 or 21. Even when students are in school, much of their education happens outside of school via new media technologies. We all know that technology has transformed our larger society. It has become central to people's reading, writing, calculating, and thinking, which are the major concerns of schooling. We want to call attention to the changes currently made by technology to learning that are, in many ways, unacknowledged, marginalized, or feared by the custodians of schooling.

We argue that technology's main impact on learning is occurring outside of school. We describe the deep, historical incompatibilities between new media technologies and schooling. Even when used at all, the most interesting new technologies have been kept in the periphery of schools, used for the most part only in specialized courses or after-school programs. In consequence we believe that policy leaders must rethink education both inside and outside of the school context.

The central challenge is whether our current schools will be able to adapt and incorporate the new power of technology-driven learning for the next generation of public schooling. If schools cannot successfully integrate new technologies into what it means to be a school, then the long identification of schooling with education, developed over the past 150 years, will dissolve into a world where the students with the means and ability will pursue their learning outside of the public school. Our goal in this book is to show how schools became committed to an older generation of learning technologies, to describe how new media technologies have unlocked exciting pathways for learning for all children and families, and to consider what schooling, learning, and education might look like in this new world.

Preface to the Second Edition

In October 2017, the *New York Times* published an article on "How Google Took Over the Classroom" (Singer, 2017). In just over five years, Google has transformed access to sophisticated learning technologies in schools. According to the company, over 30 million students regularly use web-based Gmail and Google Docs for communication and productivity. Inexpensive Chromebooks have flooded classrooms, making the "one computer for every student" dream of the most ardent technology enthusiasts a real possibility. GSuite, a widely used applications collection, includes free-to-use tools for blogging, presentation, databases, spreadsheets, photo and video editing, and distributing creative work. The Google business model gives away access to applications, creates networks of educators committed to using Google tools, and curates an open development platform (i.e., Android) to undercut competitors with powerful, inexpensive computers and applications. In return, Google is cultivating a generation of future customers who grow up with Google tools as vital parts of everyday and academic life. The article states that Google is "at the center of one of the great debates that has raged in American education for more than a century: whether the purpose of public schools is to turn out knowledgeable citizens or skilled workers."

Our book wades into the middle of the storm about the role of new media technologies in schools. We suggest that the opposition of "knowledgeable citizens" and "skilled workers" is not as clear as it might appear. As schooling moves into the 21st century, the traditional model of schooling is falling short of the expectation to prepare young people to meet the challenges of our times. It remains important to learn to read, to do math, and to graduate from school. It is also increasingly important for young people to learn to communicate with diverse audiences, to assess the truth of public claims in a multichannel media space, to produce and critique computational artifacts, and to develop adaptive life and professional skills. The workplace is changing so fast that many of the dominant jobs of the next decade have not yet been invented. Preparing young people for our world requires the development of new kinds of skills in order to become adaptive and knowledgeable citizens.

The opposition between public institutions, such as schools and libraries, and private interests is a deeply rooted principle of education research. Whenever a company like Google makes a deep incursion into the public arena of the classroom, scholars grow skeptical of the possible impact. We do not dispute this focus on protecting the autonomy and the quality of public schools. We *should* pay attention to the privacy implications of products that constantly gather personal information about young people's preferences and activities. We *should* question what is lost when companies test their products in the classroom and what follows when media companies shift public discourse away from substantive issues and toward entertaining diversions. We *should* develop and verify approaches that result in improved learning outcomes for all students. We *should* apply consistent pressure on schools to provide equal access to high-quality learning opportunities across communities. These priorities should continue to focus our activities to monitor and direct innovation toward the values that we share as advocates of public education.

The opposition between the private and the public, however, prevents scholars and policymakers from understanding the landscape of technological change in education. The role of our book is to clear a space where we can better understand how technologies have shaped new avenues for learning, both in and out of school. We describe how changes in institutional schooling have taken place in response to advances in learning technologies. We have come to think of our current school system as a stable system that resists the reforms suggested by new media technologies. However, we show how different aspects of the current schooling system—age grading, common curricula, standardized assessment, textbooks, and high schools—were formed in response to new demands on schooling. We argue that learning technologies have always acted as a spark for change in education, but that the pace of institutional change has traditionally lagged behind the development of new tools for learning.

The Internet has put a rocket behind the pace of change in contemporary learning technologies. Google is only one aspect of the new media world that is redefining everyday life for young people and everyone else. Since the first edition of this book 9 years ago, we have experienced waves of new media products, such as Twitter, Facebook, Wikipedia, SnapChat, massive open online courses (MOOCs), Khan Academy, Code Academy, the iPhone, and countless others. Each of these innovative products focuses on some form of information exchange. In other words, each of these products concerns learning. Learners of all ages readily find well-designed, mostly free-to-use virtual spaces to build and test complex models, learn to program, share creative writing, play computer games with international partners, edit encyclopedias, and more—outside the scope of public institutional access or control. Educators and policymakers must come to redefine education as a hybrid system that draws on the strengths of in-school *and* out-of-school opportunities for all learners.

For over a century, as the contemporary school system took shape, learning became synonymous with schooling. The mission of the school was to define what counted as learning and to certify that the mission had been accomplished. This book describes the time in history where new spaces for learning are emerging. Our task is to describe the contemporary landscape of technology, schooling, teaching, learning, and education. Our goal is to describe a context for us to trace the roads that brought us to this point, and to indicate possible pathways toward building new avenues that improve learning for all students and families. We hope that our story sparks new possibilities for your thinking and practice!

Rethinking Education in the Age of Technology

CHAPTER 1

How Education Is Changing

We have all heard the stories about how education is changing:

> The parents of a young mathematical whiz realize that he is not getting anything out of school. So they decide to teach him at home while letting him take gym classes in school. A retired engineer from AT&T is enlisted to introduce him to the wonders of educational software. He introduces the kid to many software programs, such as Geometer's Sketchpad, where the kid can push his mathematical knowledge to its limits. When he grows up, he represents the United States in the Mathematics Olympiad.

> Seymour Papert, a technology visionary, tells the story of how when his grandson was 3 years old, he had a passion for dinosaurs. So his parents bought him lots and lots of videos about dinosaurs. He watched them over and over. As Seymour put it, "Before he could read, he learned much, much more about dinosaurs than I will ever know!"

> A midcareer employee at Starbucks is told by her boss that she would be a candidate for advancement to a managerial position if she had an MBA. So she decides to enroll in a program for Starbucks employees for a master's degree at Arizona State Online, a hybrid university that now has over 10,000 online students. She works on courses at night, and after 2 years, she gets her MBA degree, which enables her to move into management.

> Michele Knobel (2008) tells the story of a teen whose passion is to make "animé music videos." He participates actively in the AniméMusicVideo.org web community, where he learns

programming skills from fellow members. He posts his work to a YouTube music video community, and gets 30,000 likes of his "Konoha Memory Book," remixed by animating music with scenes from the Japanese animé Naruto. The skills that he is learning prepare him for careers in the digital and recording arts.

Brigid Barron (2006) tells the story of a boy named Jamal in Bermuda, who got excited when he took a computer science course in high school. He read several books on web design and corresponded with one of the authors over the Internet. After he completed the course, he decided to start a business called Dynamic Web Design. An adult friend offered to share his office, and so Jamal designed a webpage for him. The friend thought that Jamal had real talent and encouraged him to pursue his business dream.

A teenager drops out of high school because he is bored. He decides to pursue accreditations from Microsoft and Cisco so he can work as a computer programmer. He goes online to take courses that will prepare him for the accreditation exams, which he passes. These enable him to get a job in the programming department of a large bank in his city, where he studies the banking business from software modules that the bank developed for their employees.

After she retires, an accountant decides to study painting, which had been a desire since she was young. She contacts a local artist through friends of friends on a Facebook group and decides to buy a Wacom board and start making digital portraits. After a couple of years, she becomes a popular contributor to the Reddit Digital Art thread, and she sets up a website to advertise her work for sale.

In his book *Next: The Future Just Happened*, Michael Lewis (2001) tells the story of how a 15-year old named Marcus Arnold began giving legal advice on a website called AskMe.com, where a variety of self-appointed experts provide answers to questions from people around the world. The 15-year-old had never read any law books, but he loved the law and had watched many television shows involving legal matters. His answers were straightforward, so people found them more helpful than those by the many lawyers on the site. Eventually, he rose to be the top-rated expert on the legal advice section of the site.

People around the world are taking their education out of school into homes, libraries, cafés, and workplaces, where they can decide what they want to learn, when they want to learn, and how they want to learn. These stories challenge our traditional model of education as learning in classrooms. These new learning niches use technologies to enable people of all ages to pursue learning on their own terms.

At the same time, public schools in America are facing a crisis. The public is demanding higher standards from K–12 schools, with policies that limit the variety of learning opportunities. Many communities are less willing to raise taxes for schools because a smaller proportion of households have children of school age. Children raised on new media technologies are less patient with filling out worksheets and listening to lectures. Parents worry about a peer culture where cheating, bullying and sexting are rampant, where the media market glorifies adolescent celebrities, and where school learning is belittled. On top of these problems, the best teachers are leaving high-poverty schools that need them most, because they can earn more money and respect in other districts, or even in other occupations. Many teachers see little value in spending their time helping students prepare for standardized tests that they do not think measure real learning. Taken together, these stresses have pushed most schools to follow practices that reduce learning choices at the same time that technologies widen options.

Over the course of educational history, the success of universal schooling has led us to identify *learning* with *schooling*. Passing through school, from kindergarten to high school to college, has become a badge of success for countless Americans. The pervasiveness of schooling leads us to overlook the fact that the identification of schooling and learning has developed only over the last 200 years.

We see the question of where education is headed in terms of the uncoupling of schooling and learning. We're not predicting the collapse of your local elementary school. Young people will not be forced to retreat behind screens to become educated. Rather, we see the seeds of a new education system forming in the rapid growth of new learning alternatives, such as home schooling, video games, online learning, workplace learning, web communities, and distance education, which are supported by the new media technologies. These new alternatives will make us rethink the identification of K–12 public school with the process of education, as children and adults spend more time learning in other venues.

The clash between schooling and these new technologies is rooted in the historical emergence of universal schooling in America. The early institutional history of American schooling resulted in organizational practices such as age-grading, separate elementary and high schools, and graduation expectations that protect a stable core of teaching and learning practices. These practices have proven amazingly adaptive in protecting the basic practices of teaching and learning from changes in the population, location, income, and size of school populations.

Our book provides a brief tour through the development of public schooling in America to show how the educational system changed radically during the Industrial Revolution of the 19th century. When people started working in factories, the existing practices for passing on knowledge based on apprenticeship broke down. The public schools in America were designed to offer a standard educational program to massive numbers of students from increasingly non-agricultural families.

Now we are going through another revolution, on the same scale as the Industrial Revolution. It is variously called the Information Revolution or the Knowledge Revolution, and it is fueled by new media technologies such as computers, video games, the Internet, tablets, smart phones, FitBits, and artificial intelligence. While the imperatives of industrial-age learning technologies can be thought of as uniformity, didacticism, and teacher control, knowledge-age learning technologies have their own imperatives of customization, interaction, and user control. Knowledge-age technologies emphasize access to allow people to pursue their own interests and goals. Instead of accessing knowledge through visiting physical locations such as schools and libraries, people can find information on practically any topic and communicate with others wherever they are. They also can participate in games and activities that provide immediate feedback on their performance. The promise of new media technologies is to provide rich, social learning spaces for people to learn what they want, in a community they select, and to become the kinds of people that they want to be.

The Knowledge Revolution has gradually transformed work over the course of the 20th century. Shoshana Zuboff (1988) described how a variety of jobs have changed to become much more knowledge-intensive. She describes how the job of pulp mill operators, for example, has moved from steaming rooms, where wood chips are made into paper, to air-conditioned control rooms, where the operators have to interpret what is happening by reading a variety of information displays. The work has changed from hands-on to inferential, or from concrete to abstract. Similarly, the job of secretary in many companies has changed from typing documents for superiors to handling interactions with people both inside and outside the corporation. The job of farmer has changed from plowing and harvesting to purchasing and operating machinery, carrying out financial analyses, and marketing various products. The computerization of work puts a premium on skills of accessing, evaluating, and synthesizing information. Hence, the difference in pay between college-educated and noncollege-educated people has been growing (Murnane & Levy, 1996). To earn a decent wage in the future will require lifelong learning and expertise with information technologies.

At the same time that the school system has become more focused on basic literacy and math skills, typically learned without the support of new media technologies, out-of-school learning has been capitalizing on new media tools. If we look carefully, most changes in the way that people acquire information are occurring outside of schools. Children interact with YouTube, social media sites, tablets, mobile devices, and video games for hours every day. The number of parents who are schooling their children at home, supported by online learning tools, has exploded over the last 35 years. More and more parents are contracting for online and in-person tutoring or enrichment activities. Home computers and smart phones are almost as popular as microwaves and televisions, and in many homes, children lead the way, showing their parents how to use computers for gaming, research, and networking.

As students enter the work world, computers guide their training for the different facets of their jobs. Savvy students learn early to organize their own virtual learning tools of online videos and tutorials to guide their in-school learning. And they are more and more likely to take courses at a local college or adult education program or on the web to help them improve their skills or enrich their lives. Most of these things were simply not happening in the middle of the 20th century. Technology is moving education out of schools and into homes and workplaces, preschool and postschool, after hours and beyond.

The recent history of public schooling has uncovered deep incompatibilities between the demands of the new technologies and the traditional program. Technology makes life more difficult for teachers. It pushes teachers to come up with plans for how to balance new technologies with existing curricula that school leaders and policymakers may not have anticipated. Further, the batch-processing model of most instructional programs undercuts the power of the new technologies to individualize learning. The endless amount of information available on the web—some authentic and some "fake news"—undermines people's ability to rely on virtual resources. Smart phones and video games distract students from classroom instruction. In an era of great, unreliable diversity of information and resources, many educators take comfort in stable resources that make their classroom more predictable, but may not reflect how their students learn.

As a result, schools have kept new digital technologies on the periphery of their core academic practices. Schools often provide computer labs, tech prep courses, computer literacy, and afterschool programs, but they do not try to rethink basic practices of teaching and learning. Computers have not penetrated the core of schools, even though they have come to dominate the way that people in the outside world read, write, calculate, and think. Since these practices are the bread and butter of traditional education, schools ignore computers at their peril.

The changes sparked by the Knowledge Revolution are neither all good nor all bad. We see many benefits to the kinds of education that technology affords, such as the ability of learners to pursue topics of interest to them and to take responsibility for their own education. We also see many benefits in the successful history of traditional public schooling in America, which has provided extraordinary access to learning, status, and economic success for millions of students over the course of the past two centuries. But at the same time, the roads to dystopia are open. In particular, the new technologies can undermine both Thomas Jefferson's vision of educating citizens who can make sensible public policy decisions, and Horace Mann's vision of a society where everyone can succeed by obtaining a public education. Increasing the ability to personalize educational opportunities makes it possible for learners to focus on their own self-interest and gives a natural advantage to those who can afford these services.

Our fear is that social cohesion and equity inherent in the promise of public schooling will be undermined by this second revolution.

Paradoxically, technologies that can create more equitable opportunities for learning may also reinforce social segregation by guiding users toward like-minded communities that shut out the alternative perspectives necessary to spark reflective discourse. The challenge of technology-driven learning opportunities rests on questions of access and use. More and more people with means are able to purchase the computer technologies that lead to new media literacies. One of the great promises of the traditional school system was that it would engage all students with common learning technologies. The varying levels of access and use in homes limit the abilities of schools to equitably distribute opportunities to learn. We hope that by revealing the larger pattern of what is happening, we will make it possible for society to ward off the dangers and exploit the possibilities of new technologies.

THE STRUCTURE OF THE BOOK

Chapters 2 and 3 consider the debate between technology enthusiasts and technology skeptics. We think that the skeptics are correct, in that there are deep incompatibilities between technology and schooling, but that the enthusiasts are also correct, in that education must change to stay relevant in the wake of the Knowledge Revolution. As we mentioned in the Preface to the first edition, we have been proponents of technology, and while we agree with many of the skeptics' arguments, we also hope to convince readers of the opportunities and value of technology in learning. We see the response to the new technologies taking place mostly outside of schools, and we argue that we need to rethink schooling in the light of the new technologies.

Chapter 4 puts the current debate in context, considering the revolution in education that occurred when America moved from an apprenticeship-based system to a school-based system. Our argument is that this earlier transformation of education was fostered by a number of events, but it was precipitated by the Industrial Revolution. We are now going through a social revolution of similar magnitude—the Knowledge Revolution, which is bringing on another transformation in education toward lifelong learning. In Chapter 5, we discuss the seeds of the new education system that we see emerging.

Chapter 6 describes critical differences among the three eras of education: the apprenticeship era that preceded the Industrial Revolution;

the public schooling era, which is slowly fading from the scene; and the lifelong-learning era that we are now entering. Chapter 7 considers what may be lost and gained as we face a new future for education. Chapter 8 describes how schools can embrace the opportunities that technology affords, and Chapter 9 describes what the educational revolution means more generally for society. Finally, in Chapter 10, we discuss the different aspects of education that require rethinking as we move from an education system centered on schooling to a system where people engage in learning throughout their lives.

In this book, we strive to neither advocate nor oppose new technologies. Rather, we observe what is happening, taking a historical perspective on the relation of schooling, learning, and technology. How new technologies will affect education is not in any sense inevitable. In fact, it is at critical times of change that the actions of particular individuals and groups have the most impact. The advent of the Industrial Age opened a window for Horace Mann and his contemporaries to shape the American education system of today. We again find ourselves at such a window of opportunity, where there is a battle raging between conventional and revolutionary venues for learning. There are many educational visionaries alive today. Not all their dreams will succeed, but a few of these people may capture the moment with the right idea and the right approach to change the future of education.

CHAPTER 2

The Technology Enthusiasts' Argument

Developments in technologies often have played a critical role in bringing about social and institutional change. Enthusiasts predict that the sweeping technological changes experienced in the worlds of business and entertainment also must take place in schools. Hence, many educators and technologists have made predictions as to how the processes of teaching and learning will be transformed by the new information technologies.

There are two arguments that technology enthusiasts make about why new technologies will revolutionize schooling. One is that the world is changing, and we will need to adapt schooling to prepare students for the changing world that they are entering. The other is that technology gives us enhanced capabilities for educating learners, and schools should embrace these capabilities to reshape education. Enthusiasts have argued that embracing these two ideas will radically transform the way that schools educate students.

THE CHANGING WORLD

New technologies are transforming every aspect of work: reading and interacting with the web, texting and tweeting, computing with spreadsheets and statistical analysis programs, analyzing problems with data visualization tools, creating new apps and social networking sites, marketing with social networks and digital video tools, and making PowerPoints. Reading, writing, calculating, and thinking are what education is all about.

Yet schools are stuck using 19th-century technology, such as books, blackboards, chalk, paper, and pencils. Computers are not at the core of schools. They are used mainly for special courses in schools, such as programming, tech prep, and business applications, or for basic computer literacy. Students do not do most of their work in computer environments, unlike workers in modern offices and factories.

Enthusiasts argue that trying to prepare students for the 21st century with 19th-century technology is like teaching people to fly rockets by having them ride bicycles. The technologies used at work and at school are getting further and further out of sync, and enthusiasts think that this gap between old and new technologies will force schools to adjust and incorporate new methods into the core practices of teaching and learning.

How We Think with Computer Tools

Technologies have evolved over the centuries to make sophisticated work more accessible to the common person. Some of the earliest tools, like the wheel and the plow, were used to grow crops and make clothes. The Industrial Revolution was driven by a new set of power tools (e.g., engines and machines) that were used to enhance human muscle labor. The current Knowledge Revolution is driven by a new set of computer tools that empower people's minds rather than their bodies. As John Seely Brown argues,

> Tools drive science. Not theory, not experiment; it's the tools. And it's this that has made the computer such an incredible force for scientific innovation. For example, the ability of the computer to crunch unbelievable amounts of information; to design and fabricate micromachinery; to link disparate technologies into networks; to create new materials with new properties; and to visualize what's going on in complex interaction has completely changed the speed and nature of innovation. (2007, p. 1)

These new tools are reshaping the nature of work from a reliance on physical labor to cultivating the intellectual ability of ordinary people to interact with sophisticated systems.

Enthusiasts like Brown argue that competent adults will need to master computer tools to accomplish their tasks in the future. Much of human knowledge has already found its way onto the web. People will need to develop skills to find the information that they are looking for, to evaluate its usefulness and quality, and to synthesize the information that they glean from the different sources they locate. Basic composition is being replaced by production of multimedia documents, which include text, graphics, photographs, video, animations, simulations, and visual displays of data.

Workers will need to learn how to function with these different media. Calculating has already moved from pen-and-paper computation to designing spreadsheets, managing complex databases, and using statistical analysis programs. One complex computer tool, Wolfram Alpha, carries out all the algorithms that are taught through graduate school much more efficiently than students ever will. In fact, most thinking in the world, whether for making airline reservations, controlling airplanes, troubleshooting complex equipment, designing new artifacts, exploring massive datasets to find patterns, and producing artistic products, is enhanced by computer tools. They are instrumental in all the activities that are central to thinking and learning.

Computer tools greatly extend the power of the ordinary mind in the same way that the power tools of the Industrial Revolution extended the power of the ordinary body. No one will be able to solve complex problems or think effectively in the coming world without using digital technologies. The presence of new technologies in the workplace has pushed production in unanticipated directions by creating a culture of technology-dependence and innovation. Just as reading was made necessary by the printing press and arithmetic by the introduction of money, computer technologies are changing the very ways that we think and make sense of the world.

How We Communicate Is Changing

One of the longest-running trends in history is the movement from *communities of place* to *communities of interest*. Traditionally, *community* refers to the town or neighborhood that you live in. This is the notion of a community of place. It is the only community that most people interacted with up through the 1600s. For example, in the Middle Ages, people seldom traveled, nor did they have much contact with anyone who lived more than 10 miles from where they were born. People got to know each other very well and spent their whole lives with others who shared the same experiences, values, and beliefs about the world. Communities of place rely on familiarity with folkways to make communication rich and localized.

Communities of interest, such as scientific societies, teacher unions, fan fiction writers, and rock musician fan clubs, have arisen as a new basis for communication. They are not bound by locality—indeed, many have members stretching around the globe. Technology loosened place-based community boundaries. The horse and stirrup started taking people further afield, to be extended in succession by the carriage, the ship, the automobile, and the airplane. The book and the letter began to bring knowledge about faraway places to more and more people, engendering both new ideas and a longing to travel. The telephone, radio, and television have greatly extended our knowledge of and contact with the rest of the world. The Internet is extending people's contact further by making two-way connections with worlds beyond our local communities.

Consider the typical American professional at the turn of the 21st century. Kate is an engineer at a large multinational corporation. She works with people from many different countries (e.g., Finland, China, and Lebanon), often communicating with them at a distance through phone, email, and video conferences. She has her own website, and she accesses much of the information she works with from the web. Much of her time is spent traveling to different places to work on specific jobs with other people from her organization. She belongs to professional organizations, and she regularly attends national (and occasionally international) meetings, with side trips to places that she would like to visit. She has changed jobs a few times, moving from city to city. Hence, many of the friends that she has developed along the way now live elsewhere. But she keeps in touch by visiting them—for example, when a business conference takes her near a friend's home, by phoning when the mood strikes her, and updating her Facebook page.

But what technology gives, it also can take away. The time that Kate spends communicating with people around the world may take away from her participation in her local community. She does not interact much with her neighbors, nor does she belong to any local associations or clubs, as Robert Putnam (2000) has so well documented. She may well use HelloFresh for her meals, Amazon to shop for goods and entertainment, or use the web to find out the best local clubs and restaurants. Even these tools allow her to explore her surroundings based on her interests rather than based on the familiarity of shared surroundings characteristic of a community of place. She has become, in short, a person who interacts with the world, but not with her local community. In this regard, she is just the opposite of the person in medieval times.

Kate has to deal with people through a variety of media, as well as face-to-face communication. They have interests in common but do not share the same backgrounds. Often, in fact, she may have to work with people from other cultures to accomplish projects in her work. Communication becomes more difficult because they do not share the same background, and often the medium of communication is impoverished compared to face-to-face communication. Misunderstandings often arise in emails and dating sites because many of the cues that people rely on in face-to-face communication are absent.

As Mimi Ito (2008) and Kevin Leander and Gail Boldt (2008) have argued, people are now using networked digital media for their ongoing business and social exchange. Teens are leading the way in using new digital media to blur the boundaries between personal communication, work, and learning. These authors argue that mastering digital media is giving rise to a new media literacy, which requires integrating text, video, images, music, and animation production. Teens who are creating webpages with animated computer graphics and sound, remixing images to develop music videos, participating in web chats and forums, and writing their own blogs are engaged in developing a sophisticated media literacy not taught in schools.

Preparing students to communicate in this emerging world requires not simply traditional reading and writing, but communicating using different media with people who do not share the same assumptions. Sometimes this means reading multimedia documents that come from different sources. Other times, this means communicating with people via the Internet in different contexts, such as design projects, negotiation, and problem solving. Internet communication may involve texting, email, social network sites, chat rooms, video conferencing, and shared workspaces: students need to learn to communicate in all these different contexts. Technology enthusiasts want schools to embrace the possibilities of new technologies in the many ways that are occurring outside of school.

ENHANCED CAPABILITIES FOR EDUCATING LEARNERS

Simply putting computers into schools did not produce this revolution. Enthusiasts now have turned to more sophisticated implementation models, such as the design of interactive learning environments, to spark changes in pedagogy and learning. Learning environments include computer programs where learners are put in new situations and given the appropriate tools and support to learn how to deal with those situations. Sometimes these are personalized tutoring programs, and sometimes several people may be learning together to solve problems, carry out investigations, design products, or make things. There are a variety of capabilities that these interactive learning environments bring to education that schools can't easily provide. We will consider a number of these, to give the flavor of how technologists see education evolving.

Just-in-Time Learning

The notion of *just-in-time learning* is that whenever you need to learn something to accomplish a task, you can find out what you need to know. The most basic example of just-in-time learning is a well-designed computer program help system, which gives the advice that you need just as you are engaged in a complex task. For example, you can learn to invest in the stock market by taking a web-based mini-course on the stock market. If you need to use a spreadsheet for a task that you have to accomplish, an online spreadsheet tutor can get you started and help you as you do the task. If you want to buy a car, dozens of websites offer prices, reviews, comparisons, dealer locations, lease rates. and trade-in values. These examples illustrate how just-in-time learning can come in big or little chunks, depending on the learner's needs and desires.

Enthusiasts argue for just-in-time learning as the counter to the school strategy of trying to teach everything that one might need to know someday. Many Americans spend 15–20 years in school learning things that they may or may not use later in life. In fact, we have been extending schooling gradually over the last 150 years, so that what is taught is becoming more and more remote from the time when it might be used in some real-world context.

Adults forget most of what they learned in school. Philip Sadler (1987) found that when he asked Harvard seniors at graduation, "What causes the phases of the moon?" only 3 of 24 knew the correct answer; and when he asked, "What causes the seasons?" only 1 of 24 knew the correct answer, even though these facts were taught in elementary or middle school. Similarly, studies have found that only a third of adults know how to convert between systems of measurement and calculate with mixed units, like hours and minutes (Packer, 1997). Nor can most adults add and multiply fractions or remember when the American Civil War occurred. These are all facts and procedures that we learned in school, but with no reason to use the knowledge in everyday life, most of us forget that we ever learned them. Just-in-time learning attempts to tie what is learned to its use in the world. Of course, it may be forgotten again, but it can always be relearned if needed, just in time.

The skills necessary for just-in-time learning are more skill-based than fact-based. Cultivating the ability to ask good questions (maybe in the form of a Google search!) is more valuable, from the enthusiasts' perspective, than learning a lot of basic facts. The idea behind just-in-time learning is to develop the skills that allow learners to find the right information anywhere, not just in classrooms with teachers.

Customization

One of the major effects of technology proliferation has been the ability to cater to individual preferences. People can download the music that they want to hear and the movies and videos that they want to see from the Internet. They can find almost any information they want on the web. More and more, websites such as Google, Amazon, and Netflix use sophisticated data tools to offer people access to what they might want next in terms of what they have already chosen. While major media sources still exercise significant control over what we see and hear, the Internet has loosened the hold of radio, television, and publishers on our information options. If technology knows your interests and abilities, it can provide help when you need it, choose news and information of interest to you, and explain things in terms that you will understand. This kind of personalization of network technology is in its infancy, but it will become more and more pervasive as new technologies mature.

The web has expanded to include crowd-sourced advice, information, and opinion sites on almost any topic imaginable. Google Maps and Yelp will help you find a restaurant you might like or a store likely to have what you need, along with reviews by past customers; Lyft and Uber will find a person to give you a ride; and Airbnb will help you find a nice place to stay at a reasonable price. The explosion of blogging allows anyone to publish personal and topical thoughts on the web, as well as providing a platform for people with mutual interest to share information. Cable and telecommunication companies are scrambling to create viable systems for downloading whatever books, music, or videos you want.

Enthusiasts believe that customization offers great possibilities to enhance people's learning. For example, in Charles Stallard and Julie Cocker's (2001) vision, learners will have their own computer-based personal learning assistants, which store records about each person's learning history in order to guide her or his learning. This has largely come to pass for many students through Google Classroom. Their prediction, that children growing up in a digital world will be so used to making choices in their lives that they will demand personalized learning choices, seems to be coming true as well.

Interestingly, the press for customization of learning within schools is coming from another nontechnological innovation as well—special education. The Individualized Education Plan (IEP) aims to customize learning to the needs of the individual student, resulting in a school-based learning plan that reflects the needs of each learner. The IEP represents a step away from the traditional standardized organization of classroom teaching and learning. Once technologies become commonplace in schools, teachers can build on interventions like the IEP to bring customized learning to more students.

One of the mantras of adult education is that you can't teach adults things that they are not interested in and don't see the point of learning. Like adults, young people are becoming less and less willing to learn what somebody else thinks is best. They want to decide what is of value to them. They are beginning to demand that they decide what they need to learn. Enthusiasts believe that the ultimate effect of customization technologies will be to break the mass-production model for school curricula.

Learner Control

Enhanced learner control is the counterpart of customization. New media technologies are moving control away from centralized sources toward user production and engagement. This is sometimes referred to as a shift from broadcasting to narrowcasting. In the era when a few companies, such as *Time*, CBS, and the *New York Times*, controlled the production and distribution of media, content could be controlled at the source and distributed widely, so that most people were reduced to media consumers. However, as sources of knowledge are becoming distributed, many people become both producers and consumers. In election coverage, for example, sites such as fivethirtyeight.com, politico.com, buzzfeed.com, and realclearpolitics.com bring together news from many different sources, along with their own views. These blogging/news sites open up new possibilities for participant-controlled news coverage.

Information technologies continue a long historical arc for freeing access to information. When Luther rebelled against the Catholic Church, he translated the Bible into German so that everyone could read it. He believed that individual people needed to be able to interpret the Scriptures for themselves. Luther's translation relied upon the invention of the printing press, which made it possible to distribute his translation widely to the people. In fact, the printing press helped to undermine the authority of the Church and began the long process of turning control of what was learned over to the people.

Schooling was developed as an institution to convey traditional knowledge to communities. Educators control what people learn by defining the curriculum in schools. The standards and assessment movement is the latest attempt to define what everyone should learn. Enthusiasts argue that as new technologies, like the printing press before them, enable people to take control of their own learning, people will decide what would be valuable to them and what they want to learn. They can decide how long they want to spend and what help they think they need. They are gaining more control over their own learning in big and small ways. Hence, the imperative of technology is toward more learner control, and schools are fighting a losing battle to control what students learn. Technology enthusiasts think that as people decide to take control of their own education, schools will be pressured to embrace the technologies that make learner control possible.

Interaction

The interactivity of new media technologies provides a number of capabilities that can enhance education. As is evident from the popularity of computer games, interactivity can be very engaging. Even drill and practice games, such as typing tutors and ABCLearning.com, can entice children to learn content that otherwise they might consider boring. Enthusiasts believe that by providing even more sophisticated dynamic interaction, computer-based learning environments are likely to make education much more engaging.

Interaction also allows learners to see the consequences of their actions. In this way, they have their expectations and predictions confirmed or disconfirmed and can try different courses of action to evaluate their relative effectiveness. Colette Daiute (1985) found that children who use word processors write better because they can read their typed words, whereas they can't easily read their own handwriting. Hence, they get immediate feedback on how they are doing, which they can modify easily using a word processor. Engaging in online writing activities, such as fan fiction sites, provide access to legitimate audiences that challenge writers to improve their work (see, e.g., Black, 2008; Ito et al., 2008).

James Paul Gee's (2003) work on learning with video games suggests that computer feedback need not take the simple form of rewarding or punishing actions. Complex games give users rich feedback on the consequences of a series of actions or strategies for interaction. To succeed in the games, users need to comprehend what this feedback means and take the lessons of their experience into account in future play.

Technology enthusiasts believe that when learners are given immediate feedback on their actions, they are much more likely to learn what to do correctly. Computer tutors, such as the algebra and geometry tutors developed by John Anderson and his colleagues (Anderson, Boyle, & Reiser, 1985; Koedinger & Anderson, 1998), observe learners carefully as they work to solve problems, and give immediate feedback when they are in trouble. These tutors have been shown to be more effective than classroom teaching in providing immediate feedback to learners. Enthusiasts believe that the interaction that computers provide will change expectations for learning in subtle ways that schools will need to replicate.

Scaffolding

Developing a successful learning environment often means providing scaffolding for learners to engage in difficult tasks. *Scaffolding* is the support that a system provides learners for carrying out different activities. For example, a system designed to teach electronic troubleshooting structured the tasks to increase slowly in difficulty and offered hints when a student did not know what to do (Lesgold et al., 1992). Another system designed to teach multidigit addition and subtraction modeled the carrying and borrowing of numbers with voice-enhanced animation (Collins, 1991). A system designed to teach algebraic manipulation carried out low-level chores, such as arithmetic calculations, so that the learner could concentrate on the higher-level, executive tasks of deciding what to do (Brown, 1985). Scaffolding takes many different forms, which enable learners to carry out tasks that are beyond their capabilities. In the best-designed systems, scaffolding fades naturally as students need less support and they are able to do the tasks on their own.

Enthusiasts believe that with so many students to support, teachers do not have time to provide individualized scaffolding. And students who struggle at school are sometimes reluctant to ask for help, for fear of being stigmatized as a slow learner. The recent movement for teachers to provide different kinds of lessons based on assessments of student needs moves in the direction of individualized scaffolding. But even when such differentiation is done well, scaffolding for individual students comes at the expense of other students and tasks.

Personalized scaffolding provided by computers comes without criticism, and without others knowing that the student needs help. Offloading some of the instruction onto computer tutors could support learning at whatever level students need.

Games and Simulations

Computers enable technologists to create scenarios where learners are given tasks in simulated environments that embody the kinds of knowledge and skills that the learners will need in the real world. Simulations allow players to practice risky behaviors with limited real-world consequences. Through simulations, learners may have to diagnose a disease, troubleshoot a malfunctioning circuit, or put together a television news program.

In the early years of simulation design, Roger Schank and his colleagues (1994) built a system to teach genetics by having learners try to determine if couples are likely to have children with a genetic disease. In order to advise the couples, learners had to determine which genetic combinations lead to the disease and run tests to determine the parents' genetic makeup. There were scaffolds in the system to support the learners, such as recorded experts who offer advice. Other simulations support learners in a wide variety of challenging tasks, such as solving an environmental problem or putting together a news broadcast about a historical event. These kinds of simulations make it possible to embed cognitive skills and knowledge in the kinds of contexts where they are to be used. So people learn not only the basic competencies that they will need, but also when and how to apply these competencies.

Chris Dede and his colleagues (2004) built *River City,* where learners guide an avatar through the city, trying to figure out why people are getting sick. There are three diseases rampant in the city: one is water-borne, one insect-borne, and one is infectious. They can ask people that they encounter what they know, inspect hospital records and question health workers, collect data about insects and water quality, and finally run tests to see what happens when they try to correct a problem. This requires learners to systematically collect data and form hypotheses about what could be causing people to get sick.

Enthusiasts argue that simulation is the key to letting learners explore new situations. Simulations allow learners to try different courses of action and see the consequences of their choices. That is, they can ask "What if?" questions and explore different possible solutions to problems. In this way, learners gain the ability to consider different possibilities and the flexibility to deal with contingencies. Such realistic tasks force learners to figure out what to do. They allow learners to take on roles in novel situations—something that is largely missing from school. These situations can be structured such that easier tasks arise before harder tasks.

Video games exploit real-world situations that allow players to take on new roles and engage in adventures outside everyday experience. James Paul Gee (2003) describes how video games draw players into roles that may conflict with everyday values and their own beliefs. In games such as *Starcraft* or *Defense of the Ancients,* for example, players assume the roles of different sides in complex wars. To succeed in the game, players must understand the resources and capabilities of each side in the conflict and then switch sides to take on the perspective of the enemy. Such role switching gives players the rare opportunity to see a conflict from multiple perspectives.

These simulations take on a new dimension when players interact with one another in online play. Massively multiplayer online games (MMOGs), such as *World of Warcraft,* allow players to build characters and resources in sophisticated simulated worlds with market economies and self-policing communities. The vitality of these games depends upon players cocreating the world that they inhabit. This interactive world building requires a wide range of social behaviors necessary for game success. Constance Steinkuehler (2006, 2008) points toward how these environments require advanced players to use scientific reasoning and complex leadership skills to succeed. MMOGs bring video game-play closer to real-world interaction and point to a future of how virtual-world interaction might be structured.

Computer games also excel at providing scaffolds that ease players into complex tasks. Games such as *Civilization* and *Hearthstone* strip down a busy interface to allow players to master the basic moves of game play, and then introduce more options as players gain mastery. Enthusiasts argue that the design principles of such games could be adapted to structure the learning of more traditional, school-based content.

Enthusiasts such as Schank, Dede, Gee, and Steinkuehler argue that working with games and simulations makes learning more interesting. The tasks can be made very engaging, and the conditions for applying the knowledge are clear to the students. The enthusiasts contend that this is a problem with schools, where students are learning things that they have no idea how to apply.

Although innovative teachers often find ways to embed learning into meaningful tasks, much of school is like learning tennis by being told the rules and practicing the forehand, backhand, and serve without ever playing or seeing a tennis match. Students are taught algebra and parsing of sentences without being given any idea of how algebra and parsing might be useful in their lives. That is not how a coach would teach you to play tennis. A coach might first show you how to grip and swing the racket, but very soon, you would be hitting the ball and playing games. A good coach would have you go back and forth between playing games and working on particular skills. The essential idea in teaching skills is to couple a focus on accomplishing real-world tasks tightly with a focus on the underlying competencies needed to carry out those tasks. Although real-world tasks for math and writing are difficult to re-create in schools, enthusiasts argue that simulations allow students to experience what it might be like to write for a political campaign or build a bridge.

While tying skills to practical outcomes is one way to apply the lessons of simulations to learning, simulations demonstrate that immersion in a complex, challenging environment can be a valuable learning opportunity in itself. The inherent attraction of most video games, for example, is not based on possible practical outcomes, but rather on the fascination and continuous challenge of competing in a rule-governed world. In his effort to describe the psychology of optimal experience, Mihaly Csikszentmihalyi (1990) describes "flow" as a state of consciousness that blurs the distinction between the actor and the activity through immersion in an engaging task. While parents decry the thousands of hours that children spend playing video games, players report that these simulations create flowlike experiences that can be powerful learning opportunities.

Consider the contrast of watching a student do middle school math homework with the same student playing the football video game *Madden*. Working through the math problems is often a grinding task, isolated from either applying or understanding the "big concepts" of math. The main goal of math homework is to get it done. In playing *Madden*, however, the student uses many of the same analytic skills to maintain a salary cap, guess future player performance standards, and calculate odds for success while assembling a football team roster. The flow state of game play integrates skill development and usage into a seamless experience that, unfortunately, masks the complexity of the skills required for successful game play. Enthusiasts argue that because schools explicitly draw out the subskills involved in complex learning, the resulting learning environments limit opportunities for flow. The freedom to learn the constraints of a complex world through self-guided exploration is a learning capacity that remains out of the reach of our current system of schooling.

Multimedia

Bringing together print, video, and audio into multimedia presentations provides a new opportunity for communicating information. A number of writers have characterized the shift that occurred with the invention of the printing press as society moved from a traditional oral culture to a literate culture dominated by the printed word (Eisenstein, 1979; Olson, 1994; Ong, 1982; Postman, 1982). Universal education was a product of the printing press; hence, education is centered on the major products of literate thought—namely, reading, writing, history, mathematics, and science (Eisenstein, 1979).

Enthusiasts note a contemporary transition of similar magnitude with the blossoming of new communication technologies: video, computers, the Internet, video conferencing, and so on, all of which are merging into one large network that will reach anyone anywhere. Henry Jenkins (2008) describes how new media have triggered a "cultural convergence" that blends the roles of citizen and consumer and reshapes how people interact with entertainment, work, and learning. More than just receivers of information, people are turning media into technologies of expression. We are expanding from simply "media by the few for the many" to "media by the many for the many"

(Tyner, 1994), Even though mass media are becoming more central-ized, Internet media are becoming more diverse. People are gaining new voices and new ways of communicating with the world, as is shown by the proliferation of blogs and social networking sites. These new media are likely to have as profound effects as printing, particu-larly on education, as we move into a digital culture.

Different media have different affordances and constraints (Norman, 1988). For example, video conveys sense and emotion more easily than text, but it is usually watched straight through, without stopping or go-ing back, which makes it less amenable to studying. On the other hand, computers support design, simulation, and problem solving in ways that text and video can't. Enthusiasts assume that all the various forms of media will play a role in the design of learning environments. These different media can enhance learning by addressing the learning styles and abilities of the different students, as well as by using the media that are most appropriate for the material to be learned (Collins, Neville, & Bielaczyc, 2000).

Communication

Student work in schools has always faced the artificial barrier of being legitimate only within the confines of the classroom. When student work is seen only by teachers, students do not experience the authen-tic feedback that results from exposing their work to a real audience. Insulating learning from external critique may make sense while ini-tially learning a subject. But enthusiasts believe that as student work matures, students need opportunities to demonstrate their learning in legitimate contexts outside the classroom. The development of the Internet makes it possible for student work to become much more widely available to the rest of the world. The web is the first mass medium that has open access, so that anyone can publish work in a place that potentially gets a worldwide audience. This can provide a powerful motivation for students to produce substantial works that are meaningful to the community.

YouthRadio.org is an award-winning site that provides an op-portunity for youth to report on current events through new media. Youth Radio has trained thousands of underserved students in media-related production and careers, and it also provides a broadcast outlet for youth perspectives. The site includes user-generated elec-tion and political coverage, Google mash-ups that link current stories with geographic displays, reporting on significant events on the Internet (e.g., new viral YouTube videos), and audio feeds for three Youth Radio stations. The production aspect of new media allows for channels through which user-generated work can receive legitimate public exposure and scrutiny. Youth Radio stories are heard by millions of listeners each year through National Public Radio, iTunes, CNN.com, and the YouthRadio.org site.

Citizen science is another example of how learners can participate in authentic practices through online communities (see, e.g., Bonney, Phillips, Enck, Shirk, & Trautmann, 2014). Citizen science engages learners in simple tasks that contribute to databases analyzed by practicing scientists in order to explore authentic problems. For example, the eBird project, launched in 2002 through the Cornell Lab of Ornithology and National Audubon Society, asks users to "record the birds you see, keep track of your bird lists, explore dynamic maps and graphs, share your sightings and join the eBird community, and contribute to science and conservation" (eBird.org). It supports mobile platforms for use in the field, offers monthly challenges, and recognizes an "eBirder of the Month." In 2012, there were more than 3.1 million bird observations in North America, and the data from eBird has been used in over 90 peer-reviewed articles and book chapters.

While eBird leverages the locations of its amateur and professional birders to create a vast map of biodiversity resources, other projects, such as Galaxy Zoo or Foldit, engage learners in astronomy and biology. Planet Hunters, for example, displays pictures from the Kepler satellite and asks users to look for simple dips in the light curve of stars, indicating a transiting planet. If multiple users tag the same star, then scientists take a look. The generation of raw data, serendipitous or collaborative discoveries, and solutions from citizen science projects speaks to the authenticity of these activities. Citizen science projects can help to redefine what it means to "do science."

Enthusiasts argue that the Internet offers many venues for learners to explore new identities. Learners can adopt roles through participating in online communities that have participants from many locations. A main motivation for participation in blogging or social networking sites is the opportunity to publish a representation of yourself that others will see. Constructing representations of your thoughts, preferences, and creativity allows others to identify you as a possible friend, or it can open you up to criticism from those who do not share your tastes. In either case, participants learn about what they really think and gain self-awareness from publishing public representations of themselves.

These venues provide a reason to communicate with people outside one's immediate sphere, so they provide a meaningful purpose for reading and writing and developing multimedia presentations. Although security issues have limited the ability of some schools to make student work public, enthusiasts point to how technologies create access to external audiences that can provide legitimate contexts for students to learn from how others perceive their work.

Since students are leading the way in developing new models of communication, enthusiasts argue that it makes sense to let students take the lead in integrating new technologies into schools. School designs that foster interest-based communities in schools can motivate student learning by applying their skills to new areas of investigation. Enthusiasts argue that the presence of such technologies would push schools in the direction of embracing the liberating possibilities of new media, rather than limiting its use through acceptable use policies.

Reflection

Reflection occurs when learners look back on their performance in a situation and compare it to some set of standards or to other performances, such as their own previous performances and those of experts. Reflection has received much attention as a vital aspect of the learning process for both children and adults. Donald Schön (1983) shows how systematic reflection on practices is critical for many professionals engaged in complex activities. Reflection can highlight the critical aspects of a performance and encourage learners to think about what makes a good performance and how they might improve in the future.

There are three forms that reflection can take, all of which are enhanced by technology:

- *Reflection on your process.* Because technology makes it possible to record performances, people can look back at how they did a task. This allows them to reflect on the quality of their decisions and think about how to do better next time.
- *Comparison of your performance to experts.* Some computer-based learning environments allow learners to compare their decisions in solving a complex problem to an

expert solution so that they can see how they might have done better (Collins & Brown, 1988).

- *Comparison of your performance to a set of criteria for evaluating performances.* Computer systems can ask students to evaluate their progress with respect to a set of criteria that determine good performance. For example, Barbara White and John Frederiksen (1998, 2005) had students evaluate their performance on science projects using a set of eight criteria, such as depth of understanding and creativity. These students improved much more than students who carried out the same tasks, but did not reflect on their performance in the same way.

Enthusiasts believe that technology creates real opportunities for students to improve their performance over time by building opportunities for reflection in learning environments. Using technologies that track student work makes looking back on their performance feasible.

THE ENTHUSIASTS' VISION OF SCHOOLING

In the enthusiast's view, computer-based environments promise a revolution in schooling of the same magnitude as the revolution in our culture set in motion by the Industrial Revolution. Technology enthusiasts favor a constructive approach to learning where students, rather than teachers, do most of the work.

In his classic book *Mindstorms,* Seymour Papert (1980) uses the Samba schools that come together in preparation for Mardi Gras in Rio de Janeiro as a metaphor for what school should become. Whole communities, including adults and children, work together for months to build floats and prepare elaborate entertainments. The children help the adults in whatever tasks need doing. There is much learning going on, both among children and adults, where the more expert teach the less expert how to do various tasks. It is apprenticeship in its most benign form, since they all have a common goal: to please the viewers of their floats and to win in the competitions. It is this vision of learning, but in a technology-rich environment, that Papert would like to see realized in schools.

In the technology enthusiast's view of schools, they would look more like technology-rich workplaces. Students would work together on meaningful tasks, with the aid of powerful computer tools. Many of these tasks would take them into the community. They might design and construct bike paths, investigate water pollution in local lakes and streams, build and update webpages for businesses, develop programming for the community cable television, or do planning for the town using Google Map tools.

Interactive learning environments also would provide contexts where students could tackle real-world problems beyond the scope of the projects that they can carry out in the community. They could put together news broadcasts about current events, analyze DNA sequences to look for genetic diseases, develop an animation of how objects move in space to teach Isaac Newton's laws to other students, and other activities. In short, technology can provide the support for students to tackle complex problems, which would be beyond the capability of most students, or even most teachers.

A major motivation for many technology enthusiasts is their unhappiness with current education. They subscribe to John Dewey's notion that students should be active participants in learning, sharing their knowledge with each other rather than competing to get good grades. Like progressive reformers throughout the 20th century, technology advocates do not like the aspects of traditional school, where students are supposed to sit still and listen to teachers talk, memorize the information given them by teachers and books, and regurgitate that information on tests. They think that this destroys most students' curiosity and desire to learn.

In the technologist's view, such an education produces many more failures than successes. In fact, it is becoming clear that students, who do not do well in this highly competitive system, will opt out of it in any way they can. While many progressive educators have attempted to change teaching and learning by using the conventional tools of curriculum redesign and teacher training, technology enthusiasts believe that computers can provide the kinds of immersive, customized, and adaptive learning opportunities that can reach the children who fail in schools. The challenge, from the enthusiasts' perspective, is to build technology into the core practices of school.

Technology enthusiasts envision schools where students are working on realistic tasks and adults play a supportive role to guide them toward new activities and help them when they encounter problems. However, there is a long tradition of studying how and why efforts to change schooling have failed. Skeptics have argued that schools lack the resources, the training, and the skills to change the fundamental practices of teaching and learning. Even with revolutionary tools like new digital technologies, schools have stubbornly resisted changing what they do. In the next chapter, we turn to the skeptics of technology to understand why the structures of schooling often thwart the promise of new media technologies.

CHAPTER 3

The Technology Skeptics' Argument

Two leading technology enthusiasts, Dave Thornburg and David Dwyer, put together a set of statements throughout the history of American education that characterize the resistance to new technology. They reflect the way that technology enthusiasts see the problems that they are up against in reforming schools. They think that schools are always resistant to change, even when the change will clearly benefit students' learning. [Quotes 1–6 here are from Thornburg (1992)]

- From a principal's publication in 1815: "Students today depend on paper too much. They don't know how to write on a slate without getting chalk dust all over themselves. They can't clean a slate properly. What will they do when they run out of paper?"
- From the *Journal of the National Association of Teachers,* 1907: "Students today depend too much upon ink. They don't know how to use a penknife to sharpen a pencil. Pen and ink will never replace the pencil."
- From *Rural American Teacher,* 1928: "Students today depend upon store-bought ink. They don't know how to make their own. When they run out of ink they will be unable to write words or ciphers until their next trip to the settlement. This is a sad commentary on modern education."
- From the *PTA Gazette,* 1941: "Students today depend on these expensive fountain pens. They can no longer write with a straight pen and nib. We parents must not allow them to wallow in such luxury to the detriment of learning how to cope in the real business world which is not so extravagant."
- From *Federal Teachers,* 1950: "Ballpoint pens will be the ruin of education in our country. Students use these devices and then

throw them away. The American values of thrift and frugality are being discarded. Businesses and banks will never allow such expensive luxuries."
- From a fourth-grade teacher in *Apple Classroom of Tomorrow* chronicles, 1987: "If students turn in papers they did on the computer, I require them to write them over in long hand because I don't believe they do the computer work on their own."
- From a science fair judge in *Apple Classroom of Tomorrow* chronicles, 1988: "Computers give students an unfair advantage. Therefore, students who used computers to analyze data or create displays will be eliminated from the science fair."

These points illustrate the long struggle that educators have had with contemporary technologies. For every researcher, teacher, and policymaker excited about the possibility of how information technologies can change education, there is a skeptic who questions the possibility or the value of using technology in schools. Many people who have worked in schools note that the system stubbornly resists changes to its core practices. The advent of computers in schools, argue the skeptics, carries the risk of either reducing the rich variety of classroom teaching and learning to the most predictable forms of rote learning, or of perverting the learning experience in the interests of commercial media. In either case, the conserving power of schools protects the core practices of teaching and learning from the distracting (or even dangerous) consequences of the new media.

Rather than simply concede that "classroom wins," we consider this struggle as a window for examining how and why schools have resisted past technologies, and whether the promise of the new technologies discussed in Chapter 2 will face the same fate. The arguments from the leading skeptics profiled in this chapter suggest that these new technologies will never be central to schooling, just as earlier technologies such as television never were adopted in schools in the ways that those enthusiasts envisioned.

LOCKED IN PLACE?

There is a long history of technology enthusiasts predicting great revolutions in schooling as a result of technological innovation. Larry

Cuban (1986) documents how radio, television, and filmstrips were all supposed to change schooling. In each case, these innovations had little effect on the central practices of teaching and learning in schools. Now, enthusiasts are predicting that interactivity and customization make computing a fundamentally different kind of innovation than these earlier technologies. Cuban (2001) later showed that computers have had little effect on teaching and learning in schools. He argues that technological innovations that do not take the routines and organization of schools into account will have little effect on instruction. What is it about schools that make technologically driven innovation difficult?

Public schools are remarkably resilient institutions. In fact, the organization and proliferation of public schooling may well prove one of America's most valuable contributions to world culture. From a historical perspective, the tradition of government-sponsored mass schooling is a relatively recent phenomenon. While the state has provided educational opportunities for young children for nearly two centuries, the majority of adolescents did not graduate from high school until the 1940s (Powell, Farrar, & Cohen, 1985). The relative stability of the public school system belies the degree to which the system remains receptive to changes. The American school system experienced a period of great innovation in the late 19th and early 20th centuries, but has developed a stable structure since. Over this brief period, public schools have coalesced into a robust system that thrives in diverse environments.

This model of school has been variously called the "factory model" by Raymond Callahan (1962), "real school" by Mary Heywood Metz (1990), and the "one best system" by David Tyack (1974). The model organizes and governs schools at the classroom, school, and district levels and ties together instructional, curricular, assessment, and behavioral standards into a comprehensive package of practices and expectations.

At the basic level, schools are organized around classrooms of students of the same age. Each classroom typically includes a teacher and somewhere between 15 and 30 students. In the lower grades, one teacher usually guides students through all subjects. In upper grades, however, students move from classroom to classroom so that teachers can specialize in their subject areas. In the typical school, the teacher is an expert whose job is to transmit her or his expertise to students through lecture, recitation, drill, and practice. The curriculum spells out what students are to learn, and in what order. While there is usually some effort made to customize and align curricula in individual schools, there is a remarkable and widespread agreement and expectations about what students learn when. Fourth graders learn to divide fractions; high school juniors study the Great Depression. Testing is carried out in classrooms to determine whether students have learned what was covered; if so, they move to the next grade, acquiring as they advance a record of courses taken and grades assigned.

In each school and district, these features of the instructional system weave together to form a complex system. As school systems evolved, their components have developed mutual interdependencies. Over the years, the various components of the system have settled together to establish an equilibrium that reflects a balance among system components. For example, the generic technologies of classroom instruction lead to school designs that allow teachers and students to move freely between classrooms. This in turn reinforces scheduling technologies that leave access to specific instructional technologies out of the process. The establishment of an equilibrium does not mean that the system stops moving. Rather, it means that the components of the system have achieved a balance, such that changes in the size of the student body or the location of the school are incorporated without changing the basic arrangement of system components. Once established, it is often difficult to move a complex system out of equilibrium.

The fit between practices results from many years of what Larry Cuban calls "situationally constrained choice" (1984, p. 260). He argued that the choices available to teachers and leaders are constrained in terms of (1) school and classroom structures and (2) a culture of teaching that arises in response to the stability of structures. These work together, in his view, to restrict the range of innovations realistically open to schools. The hard-won internal balance of system components provides a comfortable, well-tested environment for teaching and learning in many schools. Over time, this perception comes to be shared (and defended) by teachers, parents, students, and school leaders. Innovations that threaten the ways that curricula govern the yearly teaching plan or the tacit agreements between teachers and students in classrooms face a long, uphill battle for implementation. This is because when complex systems are in equilibrium, changing one part of the system usually results in other parts pushing back to restore the initial balance.

Jane David (personal communication) describes the interlocking and self-sustaining school system as a jigsaw puzzle. Not only do the existing pieces depend on one another, but new pieces fit only into gaps and contours shaped by previous practices. For example, implementing a new mathematics curriculum pushes against the prevailing instructional, assessment, and curricular practices of schools. Teachers may lack the training or the will to change their instruction to fit the new curriculum, which may mean that greater numbers of students fail, resulting in parents clamoring to put back the old curriculum. The existing instructional system adapts to the new curriculum in predictable ways. Teachers can regard the new curriculum as a foreign invasion into their regular teaching practices and try to fit it to those practices. Even with professional development and monitoring, most teachers know that once in their classrooms, they can teach as they please. Hence, a highly evolved, complex institutional system can be locked in place and very difficult to change.

The technologies that guide a system can be as difficult to change as the practices that they guide. Technologies that require a basic reconfiguration of instructional practice, such as radio or television, are marginalized to preserve school organizations based on text-based media. David Cohen (1988a) argues that to the degree that technology is flexible, it will be adapted to fit that system; to the degree that it is not, it will be ignored or relegated to the periphery. Here, the plasticity of information technologies works against their power to change embedded institutional practices.

While computers can open up new ways of teaching and learning, they also can be used to replace typewriters and filing cabinets in schools dedicated to preserving a hard-copy culture. Schools develop courses such as "Coding" and "Computer Literacy" not only to teach students new skills, but also to keep computers in their proper place. These offerings tell students, "Computers can be useful, but you can learn all you need to know about them in one or two courses."

WHY EDUCATION REFORMS FAIL

Schools have not been successful at teaching all children. Reformers have pushed schools to be more inclusive, more responsive, more challenging, and more accountable. A long tradition of educational reform movements has pushed schools to take on the role of becoming the primary vehicle for social and economic progress. These traditions of schooling and reform in America have grown up so closely interconnected that the history of schooling has become the history of school reform. However, while early on, the basic organization of schools developed in response to reform efforts, many reformers lately have been frustrated with the seemingly stubborn refusal of schools to change.

David Cohen (1988b) argues that the central reason why schooling is so difficult to change is the nature of the teaching and learning practices. He groups teaching with professions such as psychotherapy and nursing as a "practice of human improvement" (p. 55). These efforts all attempt to persuade clients to improve their own well-being by submitting to the established practices of the profession. Teaching is "living testimony to our faith that . . . [the] problems that have plagued humanity for time out of mind will yield to organized knowledge and skill" (p. 56). Self-improvement is difficult, even under the best of circumstances.

Unfortunately, teaching in schools can lack the organizational support given to similar practices of human improvement. In schools, teachers rarely have a choice of clients, clients rarely have a choice of teachers, and clients are often unwilling to learn what teachers have to offer. As a result, teachers are reluctant to give up the hard-won gains that come from small victories in organizing teaching and learning. Such gains, often in the form of what Lee Shulman (1986) calls pedagogical content knowledge, comprise the treasured practical wisdom of veteran teachers. Hence, Cohen concludes that teaching is inevitably a conservative practice. When embedded in institutions that protect instruction from systematic change, a conservative practice is reinforced by a conserving institution. It is difficult for teachers to implement substantially changed programs when they already have dedicated years adapting to what the traditional system of school offers.

The organizational structure of schooling has developed three strategies for addressing innovative technologies without influencing the traditions of teaching and learning: condemning, coopting, and marginalizing. First, *condemn the technologies*. In the 1950s, for example, early developers of educational television promoted innovative programming to supplement existing K–12 schools. However, the American Federation of Teachers saw the new technologies as a threat to the existing investment in teacher expertise, stating that "we are unalterably opposed to mass education by television as a substitute for professional classroom techniques" (Levin & Hines, 2003 p. 265). Media critics argued that there were good reasons for condemning the new technologies, in that they battle for the minds of students between learning and entertainment. Many schools have reacted primarily to the risks rather than the potential of new technologies. Evidence of this spirit of prevention can be found in the appropriate-use policies of many schools, which simply ban new technologies that are perceived to pose a risk to existing instructional practices.

Second, *coopt the technologies* that support existing curricular outcomes and instructional organization and can be integrated easily into instructional programs. Drill-and-practice programs can be used to support existing math curricula. Similarly, computer adaptive learning systems reinforce the learning objectives of math, science, and social studies through curricula involving progressively more difficult learning opportunities. As we will discuss in Chapter 5, schools that use these systems can assign remedial help for students who struggle to pass achievement tests with traditional class materials.

Third, *marginalize the technologies*. Interested teachers can create innovative boutique programs alongside the general school context, where they can work with like-minded program advocates and students (Powell, Farrar, & Cohen, 1985). The high school has grown through adding new boutique programs that extend the reach of the existing systems. It is relatively easy to add or remove separable elements of the system, such as adding computer courses or eliminating arts courses. However, reformers have not been able to change the very fabric of education, wherein teachers pass on their expertise to students and then test the students to see whether they have learned their lessons. Reforms to build a more child-centered education have produced only minor changes, mainly in the more flexible domain of elementary education.

The contemporary demand for standardized curriculum and assessment in K–12 education makes the adoption of new instructional directions based on information technologies even more unlikely. In most states, learning standards are keyed to both the development of basic skills and comprehensive coverage of disciplinary content. With accountability pressures rising in many schools, most efforts are going into practicing skills and covering required content. This emphasis on high-stakes measures of conventional skills and content does not encourage widespread innovation in teaching practice.

A conservative reliance on existing technologies works against re-building education around the kinds of skills for which computers and information networks provide an advantage in learning. Michael Russell and Walter Haney (1997) have shown that writing on computers can actually lead to decreasing scores on pencil-and-paper tests, even as student writing improves as tested on computers. This is because the process of writing on a computer is quite different from writing on paper. The school commitment to improvement of test scores works against the ability of schools to use technologies for more adventurous learning.

BARRIERS TO TECHNOLOGY USE IN SCHOOLS

While schools as organizations shape technological tools to serve existing instructional goals, there are several other barriers that act to prevent the use of technology in schools.

Cost and Access

Even though the expense of computers and network connections has declined considerably, cost remains a serious barrier to these technologies becoming central to schooling. Cathleen Norris and Elliot Soloway (2003) argue that in order for technology to make real inroads in instruction, the student-to-computer ratio in schools has to be 1:1. An increasing number of schools have moved toward such a 1:1 ratio in their computer policies. By 2008, the ratio of students to computers to classrooms in the United States was 3.1:1, and given the explosion in school purchases of Chromebooks and tablets since, the ratio is approaching 1:1 in many schools (NCES, 2015).

Still, a number of studies have found that despite the presence of computational devices, many teachers have been slow to change instructional practices (Herold, 2015). For many students, doing homework and communicating through Google Classroom is an everyday activity. However, many student-learning interactions are confined to these basic uses of computers. Larry Cuban's (2013) study of technology-rich Silicon Valley schools found that

> all but a few of the teachers at [the school] used a familiar repertoire of instructional approaches: lecturing, conducting a discussion, and

occasional use of technologies such as overhead projectors, videos, and computers. (p. 29)

We don't know whether the sheer availability of computers and the adoption of Bring Your Own Device (BYOD) policies in schools will begin to shift education practices toward more ambitious instruction. But argue skeptics, device availability has not led to instructional change so far.

Classroom Management

Even classrooms with computer resources present problems for instruction. David Cohen (1988a) points out that since whole-class instruction predominates in schools, putting computers in a classroom causes difficult management problems. The teacher can have a few students work on the computers at one time while working with the other students, but that can cause discipline problems, and the teacher must be comfortable splitting the class into different work groups. The kinds of individualized learning afforded by computers can disrupt the group instruction common in many classrooms. If the students at the computers are working together, they may make noise that disturbs the other students. Further, students who do not get to work at the computers often feel left out. Most traditional classrooms simply do not have space for more than a few desktop machines, and the resources necessary to redesign instructional space are already scarce. While laptops or tablets would solve the space problem, concerns about theft and breakage weigh against their use. Putting computers in labs makes managing the machines easier, but bringing students to the lab means leaving class materials behind and competing for time with other classrooms.

In addition to the space problems, there are time and instructional problems in working with computers. Most K–12 class periods are only 45–50 minutes long. The start-up costs of working with computers, such as time to get the software installed and started and getting students situated, pressure the teacher to cut down actual teaching time. Taking students to the computer lab takes more time. And unless the tasks are short tasks, such as provided by drill-and-practice systems, it is difficult to get much done in the time allotted.

What Computers Can't Teach

Neil Postman (1995) makes a persuasive argument about the limitations of computers that captures much of what educators believe. This viewpoint provides a major barrier to computers becoming dominant in schools. Postman cites Robert Fulghum's (1989) *All I Really Need to Know I Learned in Kindergarten: Uncommon Thoughts on Common Things* for a number of lessons that we all must learn as we grow up: "Share everything, play fair, don't hit people, put things back where you found them, clean up your own mess, wash your hands before you eat and, of course, flush" (Postman, p. 27). He could have added many other kinds of knowledge, such as listening, expressing yourself clearly and forcefully, and obeying adults in authority. These are all things that children will never learn from computers, and, as he points out, these are skills that we in fact spend many years learning, and school is where we learn most of them.

Teachers bring many things to learning that computers can never match. The best teachers inspire their students to believe in themselves and to work hard to accomplish their goals. They open up possibilities that parents and children may never see. They challenge learners' prior beliefs and encourage them to consider alternative ways to believe and to act. In the educators' view, computers are mere dispensers of content, and content is not the most important thing to learn as children grow up. Hence, most teachers and principals believe that computers should never dominate the classroom.

Challenges to Instruction

The innovative instruction that drives many computer applications actually makes the teacher's job more difficult. Just as with other ambitious curricula, using computers in the classroom requires teachers to put extra time into gathering materials together and robs them of their conventional strategies to keep track of what students are doing. Challenging curricula also tax teachers' expertise, forcing them to test untried ideas, often with unwilling students.

For example, Powell, Farrar, and Cohen (1985) describe the fate of the new science curricula that were developed in the 1950s and 1960s by leading American scientists and educators. The goals of the new curricula were to emphasize understanding, thinking, and hands-on activities, but they ran into difficulties because they departed from the standard school science curricula. Many teachers did not understand the new materials very well and taught by rote, telling students what to do at each step. It was much more difficult to teach with the new curricula since teachers had to keep track of all the materials and know how to deal with the issues and problems that arose in working with the materials. The College Board had to develop new tests to assess what the students in these curricula had learned, which they abandoned after about 10 years. These kinds of problems are intensified when dealing with an uncooperative, mysterious technology. Given the time and knowledge demands already experienced by teachers, it is not surprising that most teachers do not want to deal with the additional challenges introduced by computers.

Authority and Teaching

Computers act to dilute the authority that teachers have in classrooms—especially the authority over what constitutes legitimate knowledge. When connected to the Internet, computers open classrooms to a wide variety of information from a wide variety of sources. In a conventional school, a teacher controls the official information flow of the classroom. Because computers provide access to more information than teachers can possibly master, they risk losing authority by integrating computers into their teaching. Teachers earn the respect of students in part from their knowledge and wisdom, and in part from their ability to engage and stimulate their students. To the degree that students get their knowledge from computer learning environments rather than from teachers, it takes away from the respect and authority that teachers gain from sharing their expertise with students.

Furthermore, to the degree that students are engaged with computers, the teacher is not engaging their attention. Dwyer, Ringstaff, and Sandholtz (1990) report on a difficulty that many teachers encounter when they allow students to work on computers in computer-rich classrooms. They seem to feel guilty that they are not teaching the students themselves, and they feel nervous about all the talking about and sharing of information among the students. Teachers like to share their expertise. Were they to use computers extensively, they would have to give up center stage. Most would not feel that they were doing what they were trained to do (i.e., passing on their expertise to students). There are strong institutional and professional pressures that make giving up this control feel like dereliction of duty. A teacher who acts as a facilitator still can form strong bonds with students, which will earn their appreciation. But by becoming facilitators rather than instructors, are they still teaching?

Many teachers feel they are losing authority over students. James Rosenbaum (1989, 2001) often asks today's students if they have ever seen a teacher cry. Almost all have done so, even though 50 years ago, most students never saw a teacher cry. He argues that this is in part because school grades have no effect on students' success at finding jobs or getting into most colleges. Of course, there is stiff competition among top students to get into elite colleges, but it turns out that most state colleges and community colleges require only a high school diploma, and most employers do not think that high school grades matter. So unless students plan to go to an elite college, they have little incentive to please their teachers. Teachers need authority to justify why schoolwork is important for students to succeed in life. Computers can only serve to undermine their authority further.

Assessment

Standardized tests constrain how computers might be able to change learning in schools. The emphasis on high-stakes accountability testing across the country places a premium on how well students are prepared in mathematics and reading, and to a lesser extent in science and social studies. So a lot of effort is spent on students practicing the reading and computing skills needed for these tests. Drill-and-practice software can fit with this kind of curriculum. But there is little room in this curriculum for adventurous uses of computers, such as carrying out in-depth research or completing meaningful projects. The standards movement across America, in fact, is working against the kinds of learning that computers facilitate best.

In the traditional view, learning consists largely of memorizing essential facts and concepts and performing procedures until they are automatic. The practices that we have cited previously, such as the lecture and recitation methods of teaching and testing for the acquisition of facts, concepts, and procedures, are manifestations of this underlying societal belief about the nature of education. Standardized testing tends to reinforce the belief that education should be about students learning discrete knowledge and skills rather than carrying out investigations and projects.

The skeptics argue that in schools, the transformative power of technology will be coopted by the ways that schools have worked. David Cohen (1988a) suggests that computer programs that support the current organization are most likely to be taken up by schools. In fact, the exploding private market for assessment systems and data warehouses serves to reinforce the current conservative approach to standardized instruction. Thus, drill-and-practice programs, rather than more adventurous uses of computers, are the ones that schools tend to adopt. But computers stay on the periphery of the school, such as in computer labs, where the teacher can take students to practice the skills that they will need for the many tests that they must pass. *The school is evaluated on how well the students perform on tests, not on how they learn creativity or how best to spend their time.*

SYNTHESIS: INCOMPATIBILITIES BETWEEN SCHOOLS AND TECHNOLOGY

In this section, we contrast the hope of the enthusiasts with the caution of the skeptics. Enthusiasts have emphasized the transformative power of digital media, while skeptics have argued that computers have had minimal effects on schools and are not likely to be widely adopted in schools anytime soon. In our own view, this is because there are deep incompatibilities between the practices of schools and the imperatives of the new technologies. Here, we contrast the ways that universal schooling and new media technologies seem to be at odds with each other. These incompatibilities set the scene for why it has been so difficult for new technologies to have the kind of impact on schools that they have had in everyday life.

Uniform Learning Versus Customization

Deeply ingrained into the structure of schooling is a mass-production notion of uniform learning. This belief stipulates that everyone should learn the same things. Despite the practices of innovations, such as special education, typical school courses are still structured so that everyone studies the same texts and has to pass the same examinations. This notion extends beyond the individual course to the notion of a set of required courses that extends up to graduate school. The notion that everyone must come through the process meeting a set of common requirements is very deeply ingrained into the notion of school.

But one of the great advantages that technology brings to education is customization. Computers can respond to the particular interests and difficulties that learners have. If you want to learn about Chinese history or the stock market, you can find lots of information on the web. Sometimes you may even find individualized tutoring programs to help you learn. As computers spread throughout the society and the web becomes still richer in terms of tools and information, education should move beyond the lockstep of required courses and basic skills. But to do this, it has to go outside of the school, where uniform learning is woven into the very fabric of daily practice.

The Teacher as Expert Versus Diverse Knowledge Sources

Schooling is built on the notion that teachers are experts, whose job is to pass on their expertise to students. The legitimacy of traditional classroom instruction rests on the teacher's expertise as the source of legitimate knowledge. For many years, teacher education has focused on providing teachers with methods to teach this knowledge in classrooms. Textbooks are written to support these kinds of knowledge-based teacher expertise because they serve to define the scope of information that students are expected to learn and teachers are responsible to teach. This notion of teacher expertise is central to the enterprise of schooling.

In contrast, digital media provide ready access to many different sources of expertise. New media offer a variety of films and programs that present different worldviews. Before the advent of television and cinema, parents and teacher could prevail over children based on their much wider knowledge of the world. But as Neil Postman (1982, 1985) documents, that authority has been greatly diminished by what children are learning from television. Computers and networks exacerbate the problem even more. Soon children will be able to download all the videos and music and written materials that they want into their bedrooms. The Kaiser Foundation documented how far this trend has gone, with teenagers often living in an entirely different media space from their parents, and of course their teachers (Rideout, Foehr, & Roberts, 2010).

Teacher Versus Learner Control

In school, the teacher's job is to maintain control over what students are doing at all times, so students focus on learning what the curriculum expects of them. There is much to cover and limited time, so that keeping students working on their assignments and actively participating in the work at hand is the central goal of classroom activity.

On the other hand, in the digital world where children are growing up, they are free to use their new digital tools to pursue whatever interests them. They may play challenging games, put up amusing pictures on their Facebook page, write stories on a fan fiction site, create animations for their friends—whatever they find stimulating and enjoyable. But it is the school's responsibility to make sure that they are learning what they are supposed to learn.

Standardized Testing Versus Specialization

The assessment technology that is employed to evaluate students uses multiple-choice and short-answer questions to provide objective scoring. But this form of testing requires that every student learn the same thing. The standards movement in the United States is leading to an expansion of high-stakes testing using objective methods. Standardized assessments are motivated by the reform effort to ensure that all children are educated at least to a common expectation for learning. However, standardized approaches to instruction, by definition, restrict the range of acceptable practices. There is less and less leeway for teachers to allow students to choose unique directions to pursue topics deeply because this will not help them on standardized tests. Therefore, our assessment system is leading us away from any kind of specialization by students in their learning.

To the degree that technology encourages students to go off in their own direction, it is in direct conflict with the standardized assessments pervading schools. So it is in the interest of schools to limit the use of computers and networks strictly to those activities that support students doing well on standardized tests. But those are the least adventurous uses of computers, and they do not tap the computer power that enthusiasts proclaim.

Owning Knowledge Versus Mobilizing Outside Resources

There is a deep belief among teachers and parents that to truly learn something, it is critical to do it on your own, without any reliance on outside resources. Therefore, when tests are given, students are usually not allowed to use books or calculators, much less computers or the web. Tests are administered to students individually rather than having them work in groups. In fact, students are usually discouraged from working together in school and sharing ideas. It is deeply embedded into school culture that sharing and using outside resources amount to cheating. That is why it was such a revelation when Uri Treisman, who was in charge of student affairs for minority students at the University of California, Berkeley, looked at Asian-American student performance in college (Fullilove & Treisman, 1990). He found that a large part of the success of many Asian-American students came from their practice of studying together for courses and exams. This led him to set up study groups among students who struggled with their courses, which in turn led to substantial improvement in how they did at Berkeley.

The opposite is true of life outside school, where technology supports people in their use of outside resources. In the workplace, you are often judged on how well you can mobilize resources to accomplish a particular task. Knowing where to go for information or help is often the key to successful completion of a task. The web makes accessing resources and help much easier. Many people also look up information about issues that they face, such as medical problems, to make informed decisions. Technology undermines the need to know things yourself, so long as you know how to find the information and help that you seek. Hence, technology and school culture are at odds as to what it means to know and to do.

Coverage Versus the Knowledge Explosion

School pursues the goal of covering all the important knowledge that people might need in the rest of their lives. As knowledge has grown exponentially, textbooks have grown fatter and fatter. It has become more difficult to cover all the important material, so curricula have become a mile wide and an inch deep. Experts from different fields decide what should go into each curriculum, and they are in competition with each other to include the topics that they deem important. The easiest way to accommodate their ideas is just to add more and more to the sum of what students are supposed to learn.

Given the explosion of knowledge, people simply can't learn in school all that they will need to know in later life. Successful adults have learned how to find the information and resources that they need to supplement their existing knowledge. In an age of technology, they exploit the web to find the information and tools to accomplish meaningful tasks. Not only do they need to be able to find information and tools, they also need to know how to integrate information from different sources, to evaluate the reliability of those sources, and to use the powerful computer tools available to them to analyze the information and present it to others. But these form a learning agenda at odds with the school agenda of covering all the important material needed for later life. School can't take on both agendas since the curriculum is already crowded with the material deemed important for students to learn.

Learning by Assimilation Versus Learning by Doing

Deeply embedded in the culture of schooling is the notion that students should read, listen to, and absorb a large body of facts, concepts, procedures, theories, beliefs, and works of art and science that have accumulated over the centuries. An educated person is one who understands and appreciates these great intellectual products of human history. This view of learning comes to us from liberal arts education. It is our highest ideal of a cultured person, so it has very high status as a goal of education.

In contrast, the kind of education that technology fosters is a more hands-on, activity-based education. Computers are highly interactive and provide the learner with a wide assortment of computer tools to accomplish meaningful tasks. Hence, they are much more aligned with the "learning by doing" view of education than with the "assimilation of cultural knowledge" view that permeates schooling. The two views are not entirely incompatible, since it is certainly possible to embed much of the accumulated cultural wisdom into interactive learning environments, but it is not a natural fit. So technology is likely to take education in a different direction, toward design and construction of artifacts and analysis of complex problems and situations. This is a vastly different view of education than that which pervades the culture of schooling.

THE SKEPTICS' VISION OF SCHOOLING

Skeptics argue that schools will not change in the face of new technologies. The school system has become locked in place, making it difficult to change core practices without disturbing the current equilibrium. So the skeptics believe that new technology, while it will be adopted for the library or media center and for tech prep and computer science courses, is not likely to penetrate the core of schooling.

Their vision of schooling in any case does not center on technology. They think that the important goals of schooling are to inspire students to understand the great products of human thought, think deeply about issues, consider different viewpoints, and present their views in compelling and coherent fashion. Skeptics doubt whether technology is necessary to attain these goals. In fact, many see technology as a distraction.

Skeptics emphasize that schooling itself is conservative. Educators value the idea that everyone should acquire basic skills and deep disciplinary knowledge. Hence, they want to focus the schools on teaching the important knowledge that society has accumulated over the course of history, rather than the fads of the latest technology innovations. As a practice of human improvement, teachers work under difficult conditions and come to value the hard-found strategies that lead to student learning. Protecting what they know leads many teachers to suspect what might be left out with the promise of transformed practices. Further, there are many barriers to computer use in school, such as the problems that it raises for classroom management and the authority of the teacher.

One way to think about the difference between the goals of schooling and the goals of technology is captured in a catchphrase: *School fosters just-in-case learning, while technology fosters just-in-time learning.* Schools are designed to teach us everything that we might need to know in later life. But perhaps this is a fool's errand, given the virtual tools that now give easy access to so much of what is known.

New technologies, on the other hand, support an entirely different approach to learning. Learn what you need when you need it. What will it take for our society to change its concept of what it means to be educated? In the next two chapters, we look at the revolution that education went through in the transition from an apprenticeship-based system to a school-based system, as well as the revolution that we are currently undergoing toward a lifelong-learning system.

CHAPTER 4

The Development of American Schooling

There are many reasons why school, as an institution, hasn't accommodated new technology, as the skeptics argue. However, as the enthusiasts argue, information technologies are becoming central to all life—for learning and for everything else. We think that this means that school will become less and less important as a venue for education. The historical identification between schooling and learning will begin to erode as other legitimate venues for learning develop, first for adults, then for K–12 children.

Such a systemic transformation of education is not unique in history. There was a transformation in education in the first half of the 19th century, much like the one we are experiencing now, from a system based on apprenticeship to universal schooling. In this chapter, we examine this transformation as a precursor to the current transformation that we are seeing today. Just as the Industrial Revolution led to the development of universal schooling, we believe that the Knowledge Revolution is leading to a new era of lifelong learning.

The Industrial Revolution brought people out of domestic and craft industries into factories. Before that time, 90% of people farmed. It brought many immigrants to America and led to the rapid growth of cities. Horace Mann, the 19th-century education visionary, argued that education was needed for social cohesion, to give new immigrants a common language and understanding of American democracy. He saw education as providing the means for everyone to become successful. This vision resulted in an amazing social crusade to invent a publicly funded institution that, over time, promised equal access to education for all.

FROM APPRENTICESHIP TO UNIVERSAL SCHOOLING

Although a formal education system has long been recognized as a mark of a civilized society, early forays into organized education, such as the Greek gymnasium, the medieval university, and the English grammar school, were restricted to a few elite students for a relatively short amount of time. When it came to practical skills, such as how to grow crops, make clothes, or produce goods, apprenticeship dominated the educational landscape.

Until the 19th century, education was largely the responsibility of parents. Most people were farmers, and children learned the skills that they needed, whether it was reading and counting or plowing and sewing, from their parents or other kin. This was an apprenticeship system, where individual children were taught all that they needed to know by those close to them. Where people took up other occupations, such as crafts or midwifery, apprenticeship was the way that they learned these occupations. Often, they were apprenticed to a friend or relative of the family, if not to their parents. They learned by observation, imitation, and guided practice. As Lawrence Cremin (1977, p. 12) states, "In general, the pedagogy of household education was the pedagogy of apprenticeship, that is a relentless round of imitation, explanation, and trial and error. In addition a small proportion of households provided systematic tutoring and regular communal devotion."

In early-19th-century New England, Horace Mann led a movement toward universal schooling that shifted the responsibility of educating children from the family to the state. Although many primary and grammar schools sprouted up in America before the 1830s, the responsibility for education in large part belonged to the family. The early American system reflected the English model. Cremin (1977, pp. 13–14) describes the English system as follows:

> "Most English youngsters did not go to school at all; those who did went principally to what was euphemistically called a petty school (or dame school), where they studied reading and writing for a year or two under an indifferently prepared instructor. A small proportion, made up entirely of boys, might attend a local grammar school, where, if they stayed the course over six or seven years, they might develop considerable facility in Latin, along with a modest knowledge of Greek and Hebrew."

It was this English system that was largely replicated in the American colonies.

This chapter addresses why the transformation from apprenticeship to universal schooling took place and how it developed over time. Our thesis is that the American school system resulted from a chain of events that included (1) the invention of the printing press, (2) the Reformation, (3) the American Revolution, and (4) the Industrial Revolution. The last of these was the precipitating event that caused the push for universal schooling among a group of humanitarians concerned with the welfare of children in an industrial society. We will briefly describe the role of the first three precursors in leading to the transformation, and then describe how the Industrial Revolution changed America, bringing in its wake the development of universal schooling. Finally, we will describe how schools evolved over the course of the first hundred years of universal schooling.

Invention of the Printing Press

The invention of the printing press led to the widespread development and diffusion of knowledge, as society moved from traditional oral culture to literate culture. As more and more knowledge accumulated, there was a continual increase in what children needed to learn to succeed in the adult world. As Walter Ong (1982) argues, study became possible only when there were written records. Writing down ideas in general makes them easier to evaluate and challenge, and thus to be modified and refined over time. Universal schooling was ultimately a product of the printing press, and hence education became centered on the major products of literate thought (namely, reading, writing, history, mathematics, and science).

The Reformation

Elizabeth Eisenstein (1979) argues that the invention of printing brought on the Protestant Reformation. Both Martin Luther and John Calvin advocated that an accessible Bible would allow Christians to evaluate Catholic doctrine for themselves. Bibles became widely available in vernacular languages, such as German and English, with the invention of printing. One of Luther's great contributions was the translation of the Bible into German. This advocacy of reading among the Protestants, then, was an early movement toward the primacy of individually acquired knowledge over the authority of tradition. Together with the Scientific Revolution, the Protestant Reformation marked a watershed change in the status of knowledge, creating a need for new educational institutions designed to facilitate the growth of knowledge outside the clergy.

This Reformation spirit made an early imprint on American history. The Massachusetts Puritans, who were followers of Calvin, passed a law in 1642, just 22 years after the landing of the *Mayflower*, dictating that parents were responsible for their children's education. The law asserted the state's right to ensure that every child was educated. It made education compulsory but made no provision for schools or for teachers. The teachers were to be the parents or private tutors. Every family was responsible for the religious and moral upbringing of their children under pain of a fine (Carlton, 1965).

The initial spark for the movement to universal schooling was provided as early as the Act of 1647 in Massachusetts, which required that towns of 50 families or more had to hire a schoolmaster for the children. The act outlined a complete system of popular education and called for every township of at least 50 families to appoint one of their number to teach all the children to read and write, and for every township of over 100 families to set up a grammar school to instruct youth to be prepared for university. But there was little uniformity in the education that children received (Carlton, 1965).

These laws reflect a general growth of schooling in colonial America, particularly in New England. Taxpayers were reluctant to pay for education, and towns frequently reaffirmed the responsibility of parents for educating their children. Yet once schools were established, parents were quite willing to send their children to these schools rather than teaching them at home (Vinovskis, 1995).

The American Revolution

The establishment of a new country provided the founders with an opportunity to chart new institutions to serve the public good. As George Washington said in his farewell address, "Promote then as an object of primary importance, institutions for the general diffusion of knowledge. In proportion as the structure of government gives force to public opinion, it is essential that public opinion should be enlightened" (Cremin, 1951, p. 29). Thomas Jefferson, in advocating the Bill for the More General Diffusion of Knowledge in the Virginia legislature in the 1780s, wrote to his friend George Wythe, "Preach, my dear sir, a crusade against ignorance; establish and improve the law for educating the common people. Let our countrymen know . . . that the tax which will be paid for this purpose is not more than the thousandth part of what will be paid to kings, priests, and nobles who will rise up among us if we leave the people in ignorance" (Cremin, 1980, p. 108). The law never passed the legislature, but 50 years later, many of its provisions came into practice.

Although Federalist leaders, such as Alexander Hamilton, were hesitant about relying on popular education as a condition for political power, many Republican leaders, such as Jefferson, were strong advocates for an educated populace. They argued that while monarchies needed an education that would prepare people for their proper place in the social order, republics needed an education that would prepare people to make wise policy decisions and motivate them to choose public over private interest (Cremin, 1977). This call for an educated populace was not realized immediately; rather, it formed the basis for the movement toward universal schooling in the 19th century.

The Industrial Revolution

In America, the move toward universal schooling originated in New England and was spread by persuasive leaders such as Horace Mann, John Joseph Hughes, and Catherine Beecher. The Industrial Revolution, however, turned the universal schooling movement from an evangelical movement to a practical necessity. In America, the Industrial Revolution not only attracted citizens from the farms to the cities, it also fueled one of the most dramatic immigration waves in history. The application of industrial technologies to agriculture both produced the food necessary for rapid population growth and reduced the number of people necessary to produce it. David Tyack (1974, p. 30) notes that "urbanization proceeded at a faster rate between 1820 and 1860 than in any other period of American history." For example, in a single year, 1847, Boston added more than 37,000 Irish immigrants to its population of 114,000.

Frederick Carlton (1965) argued that there were only three possible ways to occupy children in the cities: (1) working in factories, (2) learning in school, and (3) getting into trouble in the streets. Once child labor laws were enacted, the choice between education and crime became clear to urban leaders. Horace Mann became superintendent of schools in Massachusetts in 1837, and he led a movement of humanitarian reformers concerned about the fate of children in an industrial society.

Mann made many public arguments as to how education was the means to make every person a wealthy and successful contributor to the new nation. He was particularly concerned about preparing the many new immigrants with the values and skills that the new republic needed.

State-provided schools signaled a shift away from the family with respect to responsibility for education. This shift did not go unopposed. Property owners, who paid the majority of the taxes, often opposed state-supported schools. This was particularly true of landowning farmers, who did not experience the urban problems of crime and poverty and thought that the only purpose of education was to prepare children for a successful life on the farm. Farm families, therefore, felt that they could provide all the education that their children needed, and so in general, rural areas were opposed to tax-supported schools. These parents reflected the beliefs of colonial Americans who "stressed the importance of educating and catechizing their children at home" (Vinovskis, 1995, p. 10).

But after the onset of the Industrial Revolution, "nineteenth-century parents assumed that learning to read and write would occur in a classroom" (Vinovskis, 1995, p. 10). This signals the shift that occurred in education from a family responsibility to a state responsibility. This shift came to permeate the thinking of Americans, leading ultimately to the belief that education occurs in school and is largely missing from the rest of life. Urban citizens turned to the expansion of schooling, often at little cost to themselves, to address the problems of juvenile delinquency and competition from child labor in growing cities. In the end, the fact that the burgeoning urban population could vote in the new American republic made it possible for the new educational institutions to prevail against the rural population.

Most people today assume that universal schooling will always be with us, but of course, most people in the 17th and 18th centuries probably assumed that apprenticeship would always be the dominant form of learning. Although long dormant, the view that education best occurs in the home, the community, and the workplace, rather than in the school, is beginning to emerge once again.

THE ESTABLISHMENT OF UNIVERSAL SCHOOLING IN AMERICA

In the era of apprenticeship, when children went to school, they attended small, one-room schoolhouses where they would learn to read and write and count, supplemented by a little religion. The early years of universal schooling saw many developments in the ways that schools were structured and operated—that is, there was extensive invention of new ways to do things. As the system evolved, it became more and more locked in place: the elements of the new design of schooling evolved into a coherent system to meet the demands of a democratic and growing society. But as the system became more rigid, it ceased to evolve as the society around it continued to evolve. Schools have become more and more out of sync with the demands of a continually evolving society.

Our focus is not on the story of how the American school system developed, but rather on how the system moved from a period of experimentation and invention to a stable system that is difficult to change. This stability mirrors the stability in the apprenticeship system, which required strong economic, social, and political forces to overcome. We think that this is an inevitable pattern with any institution, as the arguments of the economist Mancur Olson (1982) make clear. In their youth, institutional actors seek ways to deal with different aspects of their environment, and so they experiment with various structures and strategies. Those that are successful stick, forming part of the environment into which new structures and strategies must fit. Thus, a system evolves in which the pieces fit together and there are established strategies for maintaining the organizational structure when faced with changes in the outside world. Then change becomes very difficult, except under the extreme pressure of possible extinction.

In the colonial years, the towns and villages set up independent one-room schoolhouses. They were largely multiage places, with close connections to communities. As schooling became more common and America became a more populous, urban society, the school population grew very quickly. So the model of the one-room schoolhouse had to give way. Some of the first innovations were to develop graded schools, where students had to pass examinations to move on to the next grade. There was also a movement (though it was hotly disputed) to recruit teachers from the ranks of women. At the same time, there was an attempt to make teaching a profession, an occupation for a lifetime, rather than the practice that was common in the early years, where young women would teach just until they married. As part of the professionalization of teaching, schools to prepare teachers were established, the first in Lexington, Massachusetts, by Horace Mann in 1837.

The evolution that was to take place can be seen from David Tyack's (1974) characterization of the schools in Boston in the first half of the 19th century. Public education in Boston in the mid-1840s seemed to reformers more like a collection of village schools than a coherent system. The primary schools, founded in 1818 to prepare children to enter the grammar schools, were mostly one-room, one-teacher schools scattered across the city.

Tyack goes on to describe how educator John Philbrick convinced the Boston school board that the schools required a new kind of building—one that has since been dubbed the "egg-crate school." In 1848, Philbrick became principal of the new Quincy School. The building was four stories high, with a large auditorium and 12 classrooms, each of which would accommodate 56 students. Every teacher was a woman who had a separate classroom for the single grade that she taught. The students were divided into classes based on tests, and all the students in a class studied the same subjects. "And thus was stamped on mid-century America not only the graded school, but also the pedagogical harem. This system caught on fast" (Tyack, 1974, pp. 44–45).

Tyack (1974, p. 38) describes the problem faced in Chicago at midcentury: "year after year thousands of children could not attend school for lack of seats. In 1860, 123 teachers faced a staggering total of 14,000 scholars in their classrooms. Indeed, the pressure of numbers was a main reason for the bureaucratization that gradually replaced the older decentralized village pattern of schooling."

The structure of higher education unfolded in a similar way. In the latter half of the 19th century, there was a move to establish public universities. The first public universities were established in Georgia, North Carolina, and Virginia. The movement to establish state universities expanded greatly after the Morrill Act was passed in 1862, providing funds to establish land-grant universities, where agricultural science was to be pursued. Public colleges and universities were among the great inventions of American education, and they have played a profound role in the development of America itself.

A leader in the second stage of the education movement was William Torrey Harris, who became superintendent of the public schools in St. Louis from 1868 to 1880 and U.S. commissioner of education from 1889 to 1906. He emphasized discipline and a curriculum centered on the "five windows of the soul"—mathematics, geography, literature and art, grammar, and history. In St. Louis, he faced thousands of children entering the school and too few teachers and classrooms. According to Tyack (1974, p. 19), "Harris's answer was the graded school, organized by years and quarter-years of work, with pupils moving through on the basis of regular and frequent examination."

Education for small children was integrated into the system in the second half of the century. Margarethe Shurz, a follower of the German educator and psychologist Friedrich Froebel, opened the first public kindergarten in America in Watertown, Wisconsin, in 1856. By 1900, there were over 4,500 kindergartens all over the United States. William Torrey Harris embraced the kindergarten as a part of the school curriculum with his K–8–4 plan for American schooling (Farnham-Diggory, 1990).

High school provided another key piece of the system. As U.S. commissioner of education in 1892, Harris organized a group of leading educators into the Committee of Ten, charged with establishing a high school curriculum. With the exception of Latin and Greek, the core courses that the Committee of Ten established make up the bulk of the academic high school curriculum today. These courses were organized in what came to be known as *Carnegie units*. As David Tyack and Larry Cuban (1995, p. 91) describe: "In 1906 the president of the Carnegie Foundation defined a 'unit' as 'a course of five periods weekly throughout the academic year' in secondary school subjects. These 'periods' came to be about fifty to fifty-five minutes long. This academic accounting device has been so firmly established that successive attempts to dislodge it have been unsuccessful."

An established physical organization of school was also rounding into shape. In 1910, William A. Wirt, superintendent of the Gary, Indiana, schools, invented a new system for efficiently running a school, which he called the *platoon school*. The plan was arranged so all the rooms were in constant use. "For example, while one group was in its home room receiving instruction in reading, writing, and arithmetic, another group was in the music room, another in the shop, another on the playground, etc. When the bell rang, the students would shift to the next class" (Callahan, 1962, p. 129). This formed the basis for the organization of today's high school.

Other features of the contemporary educational landscape also began to take shape in the early 20th century. Elwood Cubberley (1916), dean of the Stanford School of Education from 1917 until 1933, called for redesigning schools on the model of the modern bureaucratic organization. Part of organizing meant developing a system of "continuous measurement of production to see if it is according to specifications" (Cubberley, 1916, p. 338).

This emphasis on measurement was fueled by the emergence of a strong statistical assessment movement led by educational psychologist Edward L. Thorndike. A pioneer in using statistics to measure learning, Thorndike stated: "We are no longer satisfied with vague arguments about what this or that system of administration or method of teaching does, but demand exact measurements of the achievement of any system or method or person" (Lagemann, 2000, p. 59). Soon statistical measures were developed to assess intelligence, learning, efficiency, teaching, and leadership. These measures in turn reinforced the bureaucratic organization of school management and further isolated teachers from administrators.

Many characteristics of the school system now in place were innovations made in the initial years. Others came in afterward: the consolidation of rural schools, the development of the middle school and the community college, the adoption of widespread tracking in the schools, the provision of special education services, and, of course, the development of the Standardized Aptitude Test (SAT) and American College Testing (ACT) for college admission.

THE EVOLUTION OF A SCHOOL SYSTEM

The school structures and institutions that evolved in the first hundred years of universal schooling solved a set of problems facing a growing and urbanizing country in very efficient ways. The solution that was reached may not have been the only possible solution, but it did deal with the problems that America faced in creating a system of universal schooling. Our argument in this section is designed to show how various pieces of the system were natural solutions to the problems faced in constructing a system of universal schooling, and how these solutions became integrated over time into an interlocking system of universal schooling:

- *Compulsory attendance* was the main thrust of universal schooling. The new American republic faced the problem of a largely uneducated population and many new immigrants. The goal of compulsory attendance was to ensure that the populace was educated enough to make wise political decisions, since the control of the government in this new republic had been turned over to the people. There was a further goal as well: to provide the entire population with the skills and knowledge needed to be productive workers so the nation as a whole would prosper. Finally, Horace Mann felt that compulsory attendance would gradually help provide students with the skills and knowledge to overcome the initial conditions of their lives. Compulsory attendance started with the younger ages but was gradually increased to 16 years as the country felt the need for education expanding.

- *Graded schools* were a response to the problems created by the huge increase in students brought on by compulsory attendance and a large influx of immigrants. Grouping students of the same age and experience together made it much easier for teachers to address the needs of their students. They could teach the same lessons to all students at the same time, and they could address the questions and problems that arose for the class as a whole. They could assess students on the same materials. Graded schools eased the burden on teachers. Working with students of the same age reduced the amount of curricular knowledge for teachers and made it easier for them to control classes. Later, the widespread use of tracking in the schools made classes of students even more homogenous.

- *Tests* were introduced to make it possible to sort students into classes where all students had roughly the same ability. Then they were used to track the progress of students through the system so they would advance to the next grade by demonstrating that they had mastered the material covered in the current grade. Thus, tests were essential to the goal of maintaining homogeneity among the students in each class. They further served to define what students were expected to learn, and soon they were used by teachers to motivate recalcitrant students to do the work so they would not be held back a grade. So tests came to perform a number of essential functions necessary to sustain a universal schooling system.

- *Textbooks* were introduced to solve the problem of determining what the students should learn—that is, they served to define what should be covered in the curriculum. This was necessary to provide some uniformity in what students were learning in the different schools across the country. Particularly in the early years, one of the major purposes of textbooks was to provide teachers with knowledge of what they were to teach. Many teachers were not professionally trained in the 1800s, so textbooks specified what information they should cover. Even today, many teachers rely on teacher's editions of textbooks to help them to learn the material that they are to teach and to guide them in how they present the material to their students.

- *Carnegie units* address the problem of uniformity across a very diverse country. By specifying what material courses should cover, this system allows students to move from one school to another, with some coordination in what the students learn. In particular, it allows colleges and universities to determine what students have studied in high school and if they have been prepared adequately to take on a course of study in college. In a highly mobile society such as America, the kind of coordination provided by Carnegie units is essential to placing students when they change schools.

- *Comprehensive high schools* allowed schools to offer a diversity of courses to suit various kinds of students. In the beginning of the 20th century, high schools provided the additional years needed to teach all the new knowledge and skills that accumulated since the Industrial Revolution. To accommodate this new information, the years of schooling steadily expanded, and now for most students, they include years beyond high school. High school also served to keep youth out of the workforce, which gave labor unions more leverage to raise the wages of industrial and service workers. In comprehensive high schools, some students could follow an academic track in preparation for college. Others students could take courses that emphasize preparation for work. Sprawling, comprehensive schools provided the model for the "shopping mall high schools" that aimed to provide all things for all students (Powell, Farrar, & Cohen, 1985). High school staffs grew beyond teachers to include guidance counselors, social workers, vocational educators, security officers, and food services. The comprehensive school was the solution to the problem of how to meet the learning needs of a wide variety of students.

These features of the current school system were natural solutions to the problems of constructing a universal system to educate a diverse population. The system that evolved has proved very effective in educating a highly diverse population. But the society has continued to change, while these features have been locked in place for over 70 years. So the pressures are building to find new solutions to the problems of education.

As we can see, the evolution of the American school system in its early stages was amenable to significant changes that added important services to meet the needs of a growing population. But since 1920, the system has become much more difficult to change in its key functional parts. As Tyack and Cuban (1995, p. 85) argue,

"The basic grammar of schooling, like the shape of classrooms, has remained remarkably stable over the decades. Little has changed in the ways that schools divide time and space, classify students and allocate them to classrooms, splinter knowledge into 'subjects,' and award grades and 'credits' as evidence of learning."

They argue further that this grammar of schooling has frustrated generations of reformers who have tried to improve the schools. They go on to say,

"The grammar of schooling is a product of history, not some primordial creation. It results from efforts of groups to win support for their definitions of problems and their proposed solutions . . . Reforms that enter on the ground floor of major institutional changes, such as the rapid expansion of elementary education in the nineteenth century or the differentiation of secondary schools in the twentieth, have a good chance of becoming part of the standardized template" (p. 85).

The evolution of schooling from innovative practices to a stable system of school organizations follows the argument of Mancur Olson (1982) that the accumulation of regulations and practices over time leads to mature, but rigid, institutions.

HOW THE DEMANDS ON SCHOOLS HAVE CHANGED

By the 21st century, we saw great technological and social changes that have yet to be reflected in the schools. Schools are expected to prepare students for a different world, and public policies hold schools accountable for making progress. Schools scramble to meet the accountability requirements set by national and state governments while teaching more and more students with diverse cultural and language backgrounds. We think that the demands on schools are creating the conditions for radical change, as in the 1800s, when the current system of education evolved.

The technological changes in society have accelerated some of the most profound influences on schools. The pervasiveness of television and other new media helped produce a youth culture that is increasingly complex and sophisticated—what might be called the "adultification" of youth. The pressures of peer culture can interfere with schooling. For example, the National Center for Education Statistics (NCES, 2007) found that in 2005–2006, 24% of public schools reported that student bullying was a daily or weekly problem. Another survey (NCES, 2006) found that the major reason parents chose to homeschool their children was their concern about the environment of the schools and their issues, such as safety, drugs, or negative peer pressure. (We revisit the topic of homeschooling in Chapter 5.)

The increasing diversity of the population has meant that it is often more difficult to use the same instructional strategies to teach students from different backgrounds. Immigration created very diverse urban schools in the late 19th and early 20th centuries, but the demands have changed for educating minority students for a knowledge economy. This renewed diversity in the public schools has provoked demands to reduce the achievement gaps among rich and poor students. Policymakers and parents have turned to schools as the central institution to reduce the achievement gap and provide food and basic social services, including medical and psychological counseling. Diversity increases pressure on schools to individualize education to address the needs and abilities of all learners.

Along with the political and social pressures of racial and ethnic diversity, religious groups have pressed for a schooling system that reflects their values. Many religious groups have expressed support for teaching children moral values and beliefs grounded in faith communities. At the same time, the separation of church and state and the identification of morality with religious belief among many Americans have led most public schools to shy away from explicitly teaching morality. Hence, religious groups have begun to turn away from public schooling altogether, and toward using learning technologies for their children through homeschooling (NCES, 2003).

A higher level of affluence in the American economy has fueled the ability of many parents to use technology to customize education for their children. The increasing wealth in the society has led more and more people to pay for their own educational services. This has meant increasing numbers of people paying for private schools, buying computers and network services for their children, paying for tutoring, buying books and educational toys and games, and taking courses in adult education programs. At the same time, corporations and other organizations are spending more on training for their employees. All together, these trends have led to a steady increase in private spending on education.

The exponential growth of knowledge also has put increasing stress on the schools. It is said that there are as many scientists, researchers, and authors alive today as lived in human history up through 1950. Educators appear to feel that much of this new knowledge must be taught to students to prepare them, as citizens, to make public policy decisions and, as workers, to fulfill the increasing need for technical expertise in the workforce. School curricula organized around content coverage have coped with the knowledge explosion with fatter textbooks, faster coverage of topics, extensive content standards, and extended years of schooling.

Finally, the technological revolution that we are currently going through has all the ramifications for the education system that we detailed in the initial chapters of this book. In particular, there is more and more demand for people to be thinkers and lifelong learners since technology is rapidly replacing people in the routine jobs of the society. Functioning effectively in society requires people to use a variety of technologies to accomplish sophisticated tasks. This means that there is enormous pressure on education to move away from the traditional goals of memorizing facts and routines. The schools as they are currently constituted are preparing people to live in the last century rather than the new century.

THE CYCLE OF REVOLUTION

As we've discussed, the demise of the apprenticeship system in favor of universal schooling as the form of education that we know today was precipitated by a number of seemingly unrelated movements. The printing press led to a flowering of knowledge that children must acquire to survive in the world. The Reformation leaders pushed for everyone to read so that people could learn what the Bible says on their own. The American Revolution made an educated population necessary so that the people would make wise political decisions. Finally, the Industrial Revolution destroyed old patterns of living and working, forcing Americans to develop a new system for educating youth in the modern world. These events culminated in the universal schooling system, which took many years to evolve.

There were many innovations that were introduced over the first hundred years of universal schooling. These innovations evolved into a strong system that addressed many of the problems of educating a diverse American population. But as the system evolved, it became much more resistant to further innovation. The schools, therefore, have become more and more out of sync with the rapidly evolving technological society around them today. Something about education will have to change. In the next chapter, we consider the different ways that education is changing because of technology.

CHAPTER 5

The Seeds of a New System

The history of American schooling was marked by an early institutional flexibility that has since coalesced into a system that is locked in place and is unable to adapt its core practices to new conditions. But the society surrounding the schools has experienced constant change. How can schools respond to the new technologies that have changed the face of work and everyday life?

Schools as we know them will not disappear anytime soon. Schools were prevalent in the era of apprenticeship, and they will be prevalent in whatever new era of education that comes into being. It is important that schools persist as institutions that offer equal access to learning opportunities for all students and families. But the seeds of a new system are beginning to emerge, and these seeds are already beginning to erode the identification of learning with schooling.

The new seeds are growing mainly in the areas of entertainment, information, and social media technologies and have yet to make much progress influencing the core practices of schools. As new seeds germinate, education will occur in many different, more public, and less disciplinary venues, and schools may well become responsible for a narrower range of learning.

The advent of new technologies, particularly video and computers, began in the latter part of the 20th century to create new venues for children and adults to pursue educational opportunities. Public television and the Children's Television Workshop began producing and broadcasting educational shows, such as *Sesame Street* and *Barney & Friends*, which reached millions of children all over the world. At the same time, a growing number of educational games and videos were bought up by parents to give their kids a head start. Homeschooling expanded rapidly because computers could provide interactive contact that would engage their kids and protect them from the peer culture that pervaded schools. The charter schools movement got started to provide a venue for educators who were interested in exploring new ways (often involving new technologies) to engage students in deeper learning.

In parallel with these new venues for educating young children, new approaches for educating older students and adults developed. Virtual schools were designed to provide access to courses not offered in local schools. Many companies like Accenture, Cisco, and Xerox developed computer-based learning systems that engaged learners in solving real-world problems that they face in their workplaces, such as handling customer complaints and solving technical problems. Distance education and learning centers expanded rapidly as new companies like Kaplan, Sylvan, Princeton Review, and University of Phoenix entered the education marketplace. They made their profits by helping students prepare for college entrance exams, tutoring them in weak areas, and providing courses that help adults advance in their careers. Many of these new companies struggled when the federal government began to crack down on student loan practices that they engaged in, but others are adjusting to the new constraints.

The advent of new media technologies has extended and transformed the precedents established by these parallel pathways into the seeds of an emerging new education system. The worlds of apprenticeship learning, private schooling, homeschooling, and informal learning spaces have been more receptive to the advantages promised by new media technologies. Early experimentation with distance learning, video games, and virtual curricula extended the capacity of parallel pathways, while also sparking new markets for media-learning innovation.

The corporate world took over the development of learning technologies for information searching and social interaction. Now an ecosystem of virtual learning is forming from the choice of millions of people to use Khan Academy, Google, Facebook, virtual schooling, YouTube, video games, fan fiction sites, fantasy sports, Twitter, and thousands of other options. We suggest that the collective use of these virtual learning spaces will exert a persistent pressure on schools to open themselves to the everyday information practices of learners and families. We expect that while traditional schools will continue to maintain strong commitments to disciplinary knowledge and equity, they also will come to embrace more social and interest-based learning technologies into their core practices, becoming hybrid spaces that can support the lives of students and communities.

In the following sections, we highlight two kinds of technology-driven seeds that are further redefining learning in and out of schools:

- First, we consider seeds that support the learning of school-based standards and outcomes. We consider the ways that initiatives such as virtual schooling, computer-adaptive learning, and massive open online courses (MOOCs) are creating new opportunities for learners to attain the goals of conventional schooling. We show how these new technologies have grown out of the pressure to help students attain traditional, standards-based learning outcomes.
- Second, we discuss the technologies that support learning outside the school setting. We consider the rich, interest-based social learning interactions for all ages that have sprung up around technologies that support Wikipedia, citizen science, youth media arts organizations, and video games. We discuss how the widespread consumer use of Facebook, Instagram, Twitter, and Google is transforming what we mean by everyday learning.

Taken together, these technology-based seeds of a new system have been growing in the midst of the traditional education world. But before we present these new developments, we would like to make several comments. First, the learning potential of many of these innovations, particularly those rooted in the entertainment world, has not yet been widely studied by researchers. The emerging world of technologies for learning is not only outpacing schooling, but is also outpacing education research. We hope that our presentation of these media *as* technologies for learning will encourage researchers to pay closer attention to new media tools. Second, the relative lack of research done in this emerging world also limits our ability to say much about the *quality* of learning produced in these new media spaces. Finally, we fully acknowledge that some of the seeds we identify here may never have impact beyond their initial promise. The discussion around the potential of MOOCs, for example, was a topic for debate in the early 2010s. Since then, the discussion has died down, and the MOOC structures and practices may end up being simply folded into tools for virtual education. These are the risks of trying to make sense of the future of learning and schooling!

SEEDS THAT SUPPORT SCHOOL LEARNING

Across the history of education, many options for traditional education, such as private schools, religious schools, and distance learning, existed alongside the emerging public school system. In the K–12 world, new technologies have allowed an increasing percentage of families and learners to choose homeschooling and charter schools as options to meet traditional learning goals; in higher education, distance learning and community colleges have provided increased access to curricula and degrees for a wide variety of students. Each of these pathways was designed to provide access to the kinds of disciplinary learning, such as math, science, and language arts that prevail in traditional education spaces.

New media technologies are opening up access for more people to choose these pathways to learning academic content, and the resulting increased market for new pathways is pushing technological innovation. Anya Kamenetz (2010) describes this as the Do-It-Yourself (DIY) movement in education. Choices over learning environments and pathways plus new tools amount to an emerging market for education technologies. The end result is a vibrant world of seeds for a new system that both questions the capacity of the existing school system and opens doors for new possibilities. Here, we highlight several leading technologies that are becoming new seeds for helping learners toward traditional education outcomes: Khan Academy, Pinterest, computer-adaptive learning systems, and MOOCs.

Khan Academy: Video Learning Resources for All Learners

The tagline for the Khan Academy website states "You can learn anything. For free. For everyone. Forever." Khan Academy serves as a new model for the idea that the content, pedagogy, and learning processes of schooling can be made available to anyone via the Internet. Founder Salman Khan discovered the power of videos for learning in 2004 when invited to tutor math to his niece in India. Good teachers have always realized the power of dynamic representation that lies at the heart of good learning. Khan's realization was that video could carry the power of representations across great distances and that teachers are willing to share their explanations on a platform designed to help others learn.

The power of Khan Academy was to crowdsource the creation of videos from teachers around the world. Khan Academy collects thousands of YouTube videos describing brief lessons in math, science, engineering, history, arts, finance, and dozens of other disciplines. Rather than focus on the lecturer, the videos capture a board on which teachers draw while explaining the ideas and representations. The videos are sequenced into content trajectories that guide learners through increasingly complex content toward learning goals. The videos are also linked to assessments designed to provide quick feedback on learning. While learners can interact with the videos in any sequence, tracing the video lessons through the suggested trajectories is designed to improve learning outcomes on traditional measures. A study promoted on the site claimed that Khan Academy users nearly doubled their expected growth on a state test (Phillips & Cohen, 2013).

Of course, there are limits to the Khan Academy approach. The pedagogy used in many of the math and science lessons, for example, presents the material in a noninteractive lecture format. As we will see in our discussion of computer-adaptive learning tools later in this chapter, this old-school pedagogy replicates many of the disadvantages of the "sit-and-listen" experience of traditional schooling. However, pairing the videos with customized assessments helps to make the Khan Academy experience more dynamic for many learners. Its focus on technical science and math content makes it a good complement for homeschooling parents (as well as teachers) who may lack expertise in these areas.

Khan Academy now has become a staple in many public school classrooms, as well as a tool for individualizing learning and a free resource for students to review already-learned material. Even schools and educators who use other virtual curriculum resources, such as Florida Virtual School or K12 Schools, find value in the vibrant Khan Academy user community. The range of topics addressed by Khan Academy has spawned dozens of competitors on YouTube and other sites and has led to the development of a real-world school model, the Khan Lab School, built around the idea that learners should be able to choose their own goals and pathways to achieve outcomes. Khan Academy demonstrated the viability of sites that could offer structured lessons to guide learners toward widely accepted academic outcomes.

Pinterest: Crowdsourcing Lesson Design

The dream of a knowledge repository is one of the early visions for the potential of the Internet. Sites such as the Whole Earth Electronic Link pioneered the practice of crowdsourcing—that is, of aggregating contributions of users into a publicly available knowledge resource. Now sites such as Reddit, Wikipedia, Instagram, Twitter, and Pinterest have realized the early promise of user-generated repositories by organizing and providing access to contributions across an incredibly wide knowledge and resource landscape.

Pinterest, in particular, is of interest to our discussion of enhancing academic learning environments. Pinterest debuted in 2010 as an online sharing network for users to share their favorite resources. Registered users get a virtual bulletin board, and can "pin" representations of resources (typically pictures, texts, and links) to their boards. Pin descriptions become metadata that can be searched by other users who, in turn, can repin resources to their own boards. Pinterest openly tracks the number of pins and the popularity of boards as a guide to the quality of resources, as measured by the frequency of resource sharing. The user-generated pin-tagging scheme systematically rates pins and boards that best reflect user preferences. The power of Pinterest comes from the development of social networks through knowledge exchange.

Teachers in and out of school have become an important Pinterest user group. Educators use Pinterest primarily to find and share lesson designs. A typical popular pin will include a graphic (that can often be copied as a worksheet) to describe a lesson, a text description of the lesson process and tips for effective use, and a link to additional resources. This tagged information allows educators to search for exactly the kinds of lessons desired—"fifth-grade math division of fractions," "games for financial literacy," or the "Krebs cycle." Pin rates provide an index of quality for users, and the boards of popular users become valuable community resources across the system.

A 2016 survey of 1,000 U.S. educators found that 67% of all teachers use Pinterest weekly for professional purposes (Devane, 2016). Pinterest reports 1.3 million education pins per day and has provided "teachers on Pinterest" with hundreds of boards and nearly 160,000 followers. Boards are available to support traditional academic subjects such as math, science, literacy, social studies, history, and most other academic subjects. Because Pinterest is a free resource open to the public, users are not required to be professional educators; they can be anyone interested in ideas for teaching and learning.

Like Khan Academy, Pinterest provides educators in and out of school access to an incredible variety of resources to support academic learning. Also like Khan Academy, there are obvious limitations to Pinterest as a stand-alone resource. Relying on user curation can be an unreliable measure of resource quality. While some teachers are compensated for shared resources, most engage in a sharing economy that relies on a community organized around the free-labor contributions of users. If Pinterest is seen as a complementary resource for education rather than as the core practice of professional development, it is clear how this model of open-network resource sharing can open new possibilities for reshaping education in and out of school.

Computer-Adaptive Systems: Individualizing Learning Pathways

Computer-adaptive learning tools are online systems that diagnose learning needs and customize trajectories of learners through complex domains. The dream of a teaching machine that would organize content to meet learner needs has existed since at least the 1920s. Computerization has helped to realize the dream of a system that could guide learners through complex content independent of teaching. Now commercial learning systems allow learners to control the pace and direction of their learning while providing direct, customized feedback to support learning.

In his book *A Classroom of One: How Online Learning Is Changing Our Schools and Colleges*, Gene Maeroff (2003) described the ideal of how technologies like computer-adaptive learning systems could realize the pedagogical dream of one-to-one education, where the needs of the learner could be anticipated and addressed by an online system. The learning technology marketplace of that era was dominated by what critics called "page-turning" software, which simply replicated textbook-content models in a virtual medium. In the early 1990s and early 2000s, cognitive scientists studying intelligent tutoring systems made early breakthroughs in computer-adaptive learning.

The intelligent tutoring system model required four parts: (1) a *domain* model to structure and sequence the content to be learned, (2) a *student* model of what the user already knows and needs to learn, (3) a *tutor* model that determines the kinds of feedback that the user needs to advance, and (4) an *interface* model that guides the user through the learning process (Corbett, Koedinger, & Anderson, 1997). The concept of a "learning trajectory" has recently become a topic of research as a structure that reflects how learners naturally progress through a discipline (Sztajn, Confrey, Wilson, & Edgington, 2014). Learning trajectory research promises both to strengthen the domain model and to anticipate the pathways that learners likely will take in the student model of the intelligent tutoring system.

These research programs have resulted in two kinds of computer-adaptive technologies for learning:

- *Computer-adaptive testing systems* are designed to provide immediate feedback on learners' progress toward academic goals. Computer-adaptive testing, also known as *benchmark assessment,* selects test items based on the level of prior user responses. If a student starts missing items of a certain difficulty, the system asks easier questions until it determines the student's performance level. Programs such as Measures of Academic Progress (Northwest Evaluation Association), STAR (Renaissance Learning), and ACUITY (McGraw-Hill) are widely used in and out of school to provide quick, standards-based feedback on student learning progress. Also, computer-adaptive testing technologies now are widely used in college and graduate admissions tests, such as the American College Testing (ACT) and Graduate Record Examinations (GRE).
- *Computer-adaptive instructional systems* pair assessment with learning trajectories to individualize pathways for learners through complex content. READ 180 is an example of a successful computer-adaptive learning system. The program started with research on how computers could support learning to read at Vanderbilt in the 1980s. The current READ 180 program is a blended learning curriculum based on an intelligent tutoring system for reading instruction, but it also includes plans for small- and large-group instruction and individual reading guidance. Research has identified READ 180 as a promising program for improving performance on literacy tests (Lang et al., 2009).

Products such as ALECKS (McGraw-Hill), TenMarks (Amazon), and DreamBox Learning offer individualized learning systems for an ever-wider variety of subject areas. Companies like Knewton and Edmentum are developing more sophisticated content models, for example, by moving beyond expert-structured content and toward crowdsourced models calibrated by how users actually interact with a system.

The critique of computer-adaptive testing and instruction systems typically focuses on their limited value as stand-alone products intended to replace teachers and schools, as well as their role in narrowing what counts as learning (Enyedy, 2014; Shepard, 2010). Often, critiques are grounded in the perspective that investment in these kinds of commercial products erodes the values and resources necessary to improve public education. James Paul Gee (2013) argues that individualizing learning cuts out the most difficult process for learners to master—selecting what to learn. When content is already presented on a plate, learners might be able to pass tests, but they do not learn to grapple with the difficult challenges of determining what is worth learning.

Each of these critiques has merit. Advocates of computer-adaptive learning systems typically recommend that their tools be integrated into hybrid (part virtual and part in-person) learning environments, and much of the disagreement about the value of the new tools comes down to arguments between advocates who describe what *should* happen, as opposed to critics who record what *does* happen during implementation. Despite their limitations, computer-adaptive learning tools have become widespread, given the emphasis on testing in the current milieu.

MOOCs: New Avenues for Distance Learning

MOOCs are the latest development in the movement to make higher education open to everyone. They are the culmination of one of the original alternative paths to higher education—distance education. MOOCs extend the range of distance education by integrating learning management system and curriculum delivery technologies into courses available to anyone. These courses are typically organized around traditional curriculum resources, such as texts, digital media, and assessments, but they often include discussion forums, interactive simulations, and other media to enhance participation.

In 2011, Stanford professors Sebastian Thrun and Peter Norvig launched a MOOC called "Introduction to Artificial Intelligence," which attracted 160,000 students (and much discussion!). Thrun built on this early success to launch Udacity, a for-profit MOOC provider that sought partnerships with other universities to provide access to high-quality courses for lower tuition. The Massachusetts Institute of Technology (MIT) and Harvard joined forces in 2012 to organize edX, a nonprofit group that established partnerships with the University of California, Berkeley, the University of Texas, and other universities around the world. Companies like Coursera and Peer-to-Peer University joined in the recruitment race, and for a while, it seemed like everyone in higher education was ready to take a side in the MOOC explosion.

The story of MOOC expansion is, in some ways, a tale of education hype. Its crash came barely two years after the initial excitement. A groundbreaking agreement between San Jose State and Udacity, in 2013 to provide $150 college courses to a much wider range of students resulted in lower pass rates and a nearly 90% dropout rate (Rivard, 2013). In addition, MOOCs were criticized for catering to students who already had access to high-quality learning resources, for emphasizing English as the language of instruction, and for including very limited access to instructors (Fowler, 2013; Kop & Fournier, 2010). These critiques, which crushed the impossibly high expectations for MOOCs, were delivered very shortly after their auspicious public debut.

In subsequent years, however, MOOC development has steadily received considerable attention and support across the education world. By 2016, an industry report estimated that over 58 million learners had participated in a MOOC. Over 700 universities have provided nearly 7,000 MOOCs (Shah, 2016). While the majority of learners use MOOCs organized around learning management system tools and static course content, a number of innovative approaches to MOOC design are starting to emerge. Connectionist MOOCs (cMOOCs) invite learners to contribute resources and expertise toward posing and solving open-ended design problems (Downes, 2012). Developers are using MOOCs as a medium for providing access to higher-education learning resources in developing countries, where there are few viable institutional opportunities (Patru & Balaji, 2016). As with the seeds mentioned previously, it is unlikely that the MOOC model will take the place of existing education-institutional resources. However, MOOCs will likely continue to provide a design space for educators to experiment with alternative pathways for learning.

In the 20th century, homeschooling, private schools, charter schools, and distance education have provided alternative pathways for learners to access traditional academic goals. New media technologies have thrived in the space created by these practices, giving rise to a powerful range of learning tools that are in turn creating new possibilities for innovation. These new technologies, such as Khan Academy, Pinterest, computer-adaptive learning tools, and MOOCs, may have limited direct impact on education institutions. However, these seeds are already creating the conditions for a new world of education that emphasizes the role of learners in constructing their own learning environment. In the next section, we turn to the digital Wild West—the worlds of social and entertainment media—to better understand the seeds of a new system of interest-based learning.

INTEREST-BASED LEARNING ENVIRONMENTS IN THE WILD

Surveys show that 92% of American teens go online every day. More than 75% of teens use mobile devices to get online, communicate, socialize, play games, and (sometimes) study. The demographics of online use show that 85% African-American teens get online via smart phones, compared with 71% of White and Latino/a teens. Most of these teens (66%) use Facebook at least daily to connect with peers, although SnapChat and Instagram are gaining fast—especially with middle- and upper-middle-class teens. The attention that teens pay to virtual interactions has resulted in reduced time spent with traditional television and music products (Lenhart, 2015). It also seems to have resulted in increased teen anxiety and depression (Twenge, 2017). Most American teens are growing up in a diverse digital world that has infiltrated every aspect of their lives. This virtual transformation of adolescent lives has happened within the last generation—actually, within the last 10 years.

What does this shift in the attention of young people mean for education? At first glance, it seems as though Neil Postman's (1982, 1985) critique of television as leading to the disappearance of childhood has come to fruition. Postman noted that television and music made children familiar with the adult world through the consumption of popular media. Now, immersion in the Internet has erased the boundaries between children and adults, exposing anyone to everything all the time. At the same time, though, the growth of Internet production cultures, where members are expected to make things, provide critiques, and circulate knowledge, has reframed the relation between consumption and production (Jenkins, Purushotma, Clinton, Weigel, & Robison, 2007).

The expansion of the virtual world makes adolescents the authors and regulators of their interaction, consumption, and, more important, production. Mimi Ito et al. (2010) describe a trajectory of youth participation in virtual media in terms of *hanging out, messing around,* and *geeking out,* as follows:

- *Hanging out* involves using new media, such as Facebook, Instagram, and SnapChat, to be with friends as an extension of teen social life. These media create self-regulated spaces for social interaction in a world that offers fewer opportunities for in-person teen socialization, and allow teens to extend and deepen their range of friends and acquaintances beyond the limits of place. Hanging out also allows teens to experiment with possible selves, trying on social characteristics with different peer groups, and learning about the interests of other peers in widely distributed social networks (Boyd, 2014).

- *Messing around* invites teens to experiment with the media that support their engagement and interaction. Teens mess around with media environments first by exploring new media spaces ("looking around"), and then by beginning to customize familiar spaces to reflect their preferences and identities. In the early days of social media, MySpace invited users to mess around with the settings of the environment to reflect their preferences and personalities. Since then, many media spaces invite users behind the scenes to better support their needs. This messing around is an initial step toward production, as teens become familiar with the tools needed to customize online environments. It is a spark to foster understanding how new media technology works.

- *Geeking out* happens when teens make the full shift from media consumer to producer. The changes happen as teens pursue interest-based interaction using new media. Geeking out is based on what James Paul Gee and Betty Hayes (2009) call "affinity spaces," or interest-based networks of people and practices. When teens geek out, they engage with creative tools to make media their own, with guidance from expert people and practices available in media spaces.

What do these stages look like in the lives of young people? Let's consider the way that Maya, a 12-year-old girl, develops an interest in gaming from early interaction with friends. Hanging out with friends at an after-school church club, and then through Facebook, makes Maya aware of *Minecraft*, a video game played by her friends. *Minecraft* is an incredibly popular game that, at first, allows players to navigate through virtual worlds, and then quickly becomes a game where players learn to build things. She figures out how to download the game, starts by learning to play in the free version, and finally asks her parents to pay for the subscription to support ongoing play.

As she becomes familiar with the game, she learns new vocabulary and game-play strategies. She learns that "mobs" are in-game characters that have predictable properties, and she hears about special mobs, called "creepers," who sneak up on players and blow up whatever players are building. Learning the discourse of the game begins to shape how she hangs out with her friends. She listens more closely to friends who play *Minecraft* all the time. One friend, Sarah, posts videos on YouTube about the buildings that she is constructing. Maya doesn't know how this works, but she is impressed by her friend's technical ability. Sarah shows Maya an online YouTube community of *Minecraft* players who talk about messing with the settings to customize the game.

Maya begins watching the *Minecraft* YouTube videos (instead of television) and learns more about how players interact in this virtual affinity space. She also discovers that she likes to use *Minecraft* as a "sandbox," an open design space where she can make models of the buildings in her real-life world. She learns how to open the command prompt line in the game, which allows players to mess around with the game settings, and how to use "cheats" to get more resources and more lives in the game. Players on YouTube rely on cheats and the command line interface to remake the game to suit their own goals and styles of play. After fooling around for several months with the tips provided by the YouTube affinity space, Maya is beginning to develop her own style of play and plan how she would like the game to work.

After Maya watches a classic science fiction movie with her dad, *The Fifth Element,* she is inspired by the architecture from the movie and wants to create *Minecraft* buildings modeled on it. This is where Ito's geeking-out stage blossoms for Maya. She finds a YouTube channel where players re-create scenes from famous sci-fi movies and begins to play with tools that allow players to capture and narrate *Minecraft* event sequences and edit the footage into short movies. Maya needs to dive into user communities dedicated to "modding," or using in-game design tools to modify the game world to reflect her plans. She consults sites that describe how to use an in-game camera to capture her new landscape and to build characters who could re-enact scenes from the movie. As she develops her own content, she begins to give feedback on the YouTube videos that she has watched, posts her own videos, gains a number of followers for her own channel, and begins to answer questions about technical processes posed by other users. As Maya geeks out on this new activity of producing movies from *Minecraft,* she completes the cycle of consumption to production that characterizes so much of youth experience with new media environments.

The hanging out/messing around/geeking out cycle is widely experienced as a process of informal learning with new media spaces. It shapes out-of-school learning not only for youth, but for learners of all ages. Affinity groups are available online for almost any topic, are typically accessible as knowledge resources to newcomers and casual browsers, and are articulated into production communities for a smaller number of users. Maya's example shows how new media environments facilitate learners' transitions from consumers to producers of information and products.

In the following sections, we highlight how the worlds of Wikipedia and YouTube support learners across Ito's trajectory.

Wikipedia: The World's Biggest Collaborative Writing Project

With nearly 400 million views per day, Wikipedia includes more than 46 million articles in 299 languages, including 5.5 million in English. There are 70,000 active writers who work on thousands of pages per day and delete 1,000 obsolete pages every day. Guided by the *Wikipedia Manual of Style,* this collection of writers from across the world is the biggest collaborative writing project in human history.

Wikipedia was founded in 2001. In the early years, Wikipedia entries were often criticized for accuracy by teachers and librarians.

Since then, the quality of the entries has been shown to rival the *Encyclopedia Britannica,* and the scope of Wikipedia articles greatly surpasses any other encyclopedia source (Giles, 2005). Like Facebook and Google, Wikipedia has spawned a vocabulary and technology of its own (the wiki) as the name for a network of tools that support asynchronous user contributions and collaboration through simple text editors and threaded contributions.

Wikipedia is a basic knowledge resource for most users. Casual users search Wikipedia while hanging out online to resolve arguments or answer questions. Getting caught in a Wikipedia browsing vortex is the 21st-century equivalent of getting lost in the public library stacks. The transition from consuming to producing Wiki articles has been made seamless over the years. Registering as a Wiki editor is easy, and an army of amateur editors regularly review all changes that are made by new editors. The open editing environment of the Wiki invites users to make corrections in articles when mistakes are spotted. Messing around with Wikipedia means experimenting with editing tools, establishing a user profile, and submitting changes for review by expert editors.

When users get captured by the spirit of the collective editing at a global scale, they can geek out by joining the expert editor game. Editors gain expertise by earning more control over the content of pages, ascending from confirmed users, to administrators, to bureaucrats who are allowed to control the accounts of other users. Scoreboards of the number and quality of edits performed rate the contributions of individual editors. Wikipedia and the tools and community that it sparked are powerful seeds for organizing and distributing user-produced knowledge and community structures across formal and informal learning environments.

YouTube: Watching, Making, and Sharing Videos for Everyone

YouTube is the biggest video-sharing site in the world. Started in 2005, it allows users to view videos, but it also provides free, easy-to-use tools for uploading content and maintaining user accounts. YouTube has been part of Google since 2006, and like Wikipedia, it has become a widely used noun and verb. Most of the videos on YouTube are available for free to any users, including Khan Academy and the game-play scenarios mentioned previously. More than 400 hours of content are uploaded to YouTube every minute, and 1 billion hours of content are watched every day on the site.

YouTube has become one of the primary pathways for informal learning on the Internet. How-to videos, documentaries, newscasts, vintage sporting events, and nearly every kind of video ever recorded are available for free or via subscription on YouTube. Millennials spend twice as much time watching YouTube as television (Williams, 2016). The viewing habits of young people have created stars built on the number of subscribers and likes on YouTube. Celebrities such as PewDiePie, who plays and comments on video games, has 54 million subscribers and earns, through ad support, over $15 million per year. Other YouTube stars use comedy, guests, and rapid-fire commentary to generate millions of viewers.

The self-made status of these new media YouTube stars has inspired a generation of young people to mess around and geek out to become YouTube stars of their own. YouTube's internal pricing structure rewards ad revenue to users who generate a sufficient level of likes and subscriptions. YouTube has become a gigantic affinity space for young users who watch their favorites, produce their own videos, generate feedback, and improve their video creation craft. Any young person with a smart phone can enter this affinity space, rich with guidance on pacing, editing, narrative, comedy, special effects, transitions, publicity, and marketing strategies.

The sheer number of users on sites like YouTube (1.3 billion active users), Reddit (542 million monthly), Twitter (328 million monthly), Instagram (500 million daily), and SnapChat (150 million daily) demonstrates the footprint that new media sites have on daily life. Each site offers pathways for users to transition from consumers to producers of opinions, photos, memes, and commentary. The variety of these kinds of sites results in an unwieldy, decentered media world vulnerable to fragmentation in ways that prevent the emergence of shared understanding, or even shared recognition of what counts as facts. From a learning perspective, though, each of these sites traces a clear pathway for users to learn not only the presented content, but also how to use open-source tools to produce and circulate content of their own. Like Wikipedia, YouTube and similar sites provide ample evidence that new media are powerful tools that define new pathways for learning outside of school.

Maker Spaces: Building in the Material World

The final example of popular, interest-based learning environments in this chapter is not a virtual space, but an open-source place for technical and craft learning (Halverson, Kallio, Hackett, & Halverson, 2016). Maker spaces, also known as *hacker spaces* and, in some cases, *FabLabs*, "are informal sites for creative production in art, science, and engineering, where people of all ages blend digital and physical technologies to explore ideas, learn technical skills, and create new products" (Sheridan et al., 2014, p. 505). Maker spaces are shared, public spaces for people to come together, build stuff, and exchange ideas.

Some maker spaces focus on coding and circuitry, others on music and media making, and still others on ceramics, knitting, and sewing arts. These spaces usually include short-term classes and communities of makers of different ability levels, who engage in a variety of projects in which veterans are expected to help novices use tools and think through projects. Over time, a successful maker space develops a culture that both encourages new participants to learn to create things and provides expert makers a shared space for working on long-term projects.

Maker spaces have become an international movement. Almost 1,500 maker spaces operate around the world, and libraries, museums, schools, and community centers are adding sites every month (Lou & Peck, 2016). Some maker spaces are housed in public institutions such as libraries and schools or fee-based institutions such as museums; others are stand-alone spaces dedicated to various forms of making, independent of institutional affiliation. Some maker spaces offer free access for users to explore and to engage in projects; others require a membership fee or a commitment to serve as a mentor for new makers.

Many maker communities originated in the open-source world that formed around creating and patching software. FabLabs, one of the earliest organized forms of maker spaces for digital fabrication, were sparked by Neil Gershenfeld's (2012) work at MIT in the early 2000s. FabLabs allow everyday people to build solutions to their own problems using a package of tools and plans to teach engineering, robotics, design, and programming. Nearly 500 FabLabs operate around the world, and FabLabs have been adapted for use in K–12 schools worldwide.

A key affordance of maker spaces, based on the FabLab model, is access to an open, user-generated network of blueprints (on sites such as thingiverse.com or instructables.com) to design anything from furniture to power generators. Organizations like Maker Media provide access to blueprints through websites and conventional publications (*Make* magazine), as well as national user communities through Maker Faires—more than 120,000 people attended the 2016 Bay Area Maker Faire (Conlan, 2016).

Youth media arts organizations (YMAOs) are special kinds of maker spaces that specialize in digital audio and video making. They invite youth to learn how to use media tools to produce digital art such as movies, music, and podcasts about their lives and their world. YMAOs typically flourish in out-of-school contexts, where production and performance artists can work with youth in a collaborative design environment. These organizations typically include virtual channels that allow for the distribution of products, where authentic audiences can provide critique and promotion (Halverson, Lowenhaupt, Gibbons, & Bass, 2009).

The Chicago Digital Youth Network is an example of the design and durability of a YMAO. Started in 2005, the network grew from an afterschool program to a MacArthur Foundation–funded partnership with Chicago Public Libraries to create a space for urban youth to engage in media arts (Barron, Gomez, Pinkard, & Martin, 2014). Network members create music, videos, and stories inspired by their experiences and by ideas generated in workshops with peers and mentors. Each member uses an online environment to access learning resources and mentorship. The process, guided by mentors in real-world arts communities, shapes social interaction around creating things into a genuine participatory culture. YMAOs such as YouthRadio (youthradio.org), AppalShop (appalshop.org), ReelWorks (reelworks.org), and InProgress (in-progress.org) share similar structures to guide young people in making sophisticated media about their lives and communities (Black, 2008; Chau, 2010). Maker spaces such as YMAOs provide a physical space and access to resources that organize and support the development of new literacies through production.

Maker spaces provide a viable model to spark interest-based learning anywhere. Makers hang out with like-minded peers, experimenting with tools and attending beginning workshops, as a way to become familiar with community practices. They mess around with tools on projects of their own to explore what can be done in a given medium and to acquire new forms of technical skill. Once inducted into the basics of the art form, makers geek out by creating in terms of the standards and practices of the medium, by innovating on these standards and practices, and through helping others in the emergent community of practice.

New media technologies such as video games, Wikipedia, YouTube, and maker spaces open entirely new avenues for interest-based learning. Prior to the Internet, the range of interest-based learning was limited to the people in the local community and the books in the public library. In communities where everyone shared the same interests and where the library budget was small, the range of possible interests to pursue was constrained.

Not only does access to the Internet exponentially increase the range of topics available to pursue, but the new media tools that organize the content also help users construct virtual social environments to facilitate learning. As Mimi Ito et al. (2010) suggest, these kinds of virtual environments have given rise to a sequence of informal stages that allow learners to build on their interests in order to advance from consumers to producers of knowledge.

CONCLUSION

Our goal in this chapter was to highlight some of the seeds of a new system of education developing in our midst. In the previous chapter, we argued that the existing public school systems adapted to meet the requirements to provide education for all children in the 20th century. However, like many successful institutions, the core structures of public schooling hardened and became inflexible as schools addressed the needs of more communities and families. Now, in the 21st century, as the challenges of learning are changing with the advent of new media information technologies, many schools have found it difficult to adapt to welcoming new tools into core practices.

As a result, the lives of students, families, and educators are split between the technologies that support the core practices of schools and the technologies used in everyday life. In this chapter, we described how new media technologies are creating new pathways for learning. Tools like Khan Academy, Pinterest, computer-adaptive learning systems, and MOOCs exploit opportunities in existing school practices to encourage learners to meet traditional, school-based learning goals. Tools such as video games, Wikipedia, YouTube, and maker spaces facilitate an extraordinary range of interest-based learning goals, as defined by learners themselves. Individually, each of these tools can be seen as a means to achieve system-defined or learner-defined outcomes. But taken together, we can see how the Internet has become an incubator for a radical expansion in what counts as a learning environment that blends the formal, institutional setting for schooling with informal, out-of-school occasions for learning. If the goal of the next generation of schooling is to create 21st-century learners who are motivated to seek out and solve complex problems, these new media tools will be critical elements of an emerging new system of schooling.

CHAPTER 6

The Three Eras of Education

The seeds of a new system are thriving as we enter into a new era of education for lifelong learning. Having experienced the apprenticeship and universal-schooling eras, the technological advances that formed the seeds of a new system are bringing this new era into being. These three eras differ in many aspects. In some ways, the lifelong learning era seems to reflect elements of the earlier apprenticeship era.

As we moved from the apprenticeship era to the universal-schooling era, changes took place in a number of different dimensions: who was responsible for children's education, what the purpose and content of their education were, how students were to be taught and assessed, and what we expected them to learn. There were also changes in the location of where the learning occurred, the culture in which learning occurred, and the relationships between teachers and learners. All these aspects of education are changing once again as we move into the era of lifelong learning.

RESPONSIBILITY: FROM PARENTS TO THE STATE, THEN TO INDIVIDUALS AND PARENTS AGAIN

Perhaps the most revolutionary idea advanced by Horace Mann and his colleagues was for the state to take over responsibility for educating children from their parents. In the apprenticeship era, parents decided what their children would learn. Parents would often decide what occupation a boy would pursue, and either the father would train him if he were to follow in the father's footsteps, or the boy would be apprenticed to a relative or friend to learn a trade. Girls learned their household and other duties from their mothers. If they lived on a farm, as was most common, mothers would teach the girls their farm duties, such as milking cows. If the family were in a trade, the mother often would run the shop, and the girls would learn how to do that. If the mother were a midwife, the girls would learn midwifery by observing their mother and slowly helping and taking on some of her responsibilities. Many of the learned people in the apprenticeship era were largely self-taught, as the story of Abraham Lincoln reading at night by the fire illustrates.

With the onset of the Industrial Revolution, there was a concern about immigrant children learning the values and language of America, and a sense that this would be the responsibility of the state, not of parents. The reformers felt that schools were needed to teach American values to immigrant children. So they advocated taking control of education from the parents and giving it to the state. This often led to children developing attitudes and values that their parents did not share. A graphic description of this process is beautifully described in Richard Rodriguez's (1982) autobiographical book, *Hunger of Memory: The Education of Richard Rodriguez*, where he describes how he was torn between his parents' values and the American values that he acquired from his schooling.

In the present lifelong-learning era, responsibility for education is shifting away from the state and back to the parents (for younger children) and to the individual (for teenagers and adults). This movement reflects the emphasis on customizing education to the particular learners' needs, interests, and abilities. We see this in the growth of the seeds of a new system, as described in Chapter 5. More and more parents are taking control of the education of their children through homeschooling, using supports such as Khan Academy and computer tools, by teaching them values that they think are important, and by investing in summer camps and afterschool activities to support their interests. After the college years, increasing numbers of adults pursue opportunities to advance their careers and develop their deep interests. This movement toward Do-It-Yourself (DIY) learning is beginning in the teen years, outside of high school. Bill Gates is famous for spending many hours during his high school years programming computers. While high schools offer some choices, technology makes it easier for teens, as well as adults, to pursue their individual passions in affinity groups, often accessed online.

EXPECTATIONS: FROM SOCIAL REPRODUCTION TO SUCCESS FOR ALL TO INDIVIDUAL CHOICE

As noted previously, before the Industrial Revolution, parents wanted their children to follow in their footsteps. Therefore, the education that they expected for their children was the same education that they had acquired. If they were farmers, the children were expected to learn to be farmers. If they were engaged in trade or a craft, their children were expected to learn to carry on that trade or craft. If they read the Bible, children were expected to learn to read.

These expectations supported the reproduction of class differences. There was little room for social mobility, which would allow children to advance themselves by getting a good education. Even when parents pursued better opportunities for their children, the custodians of the existing class structure created little room for advancement. The lack of overall economic growth created the assumption of social stability, where children would face a world much like the one that their parents had faced. So the goal was to raise children with the same skills that their parents had.

After the Industrial Revolution, the opening up of economic opportunity and social mobility, especially among immigrant Americans, gave rise to an increasing appetite for real social mobility. Horace Mann argued that education could be the ladder to a common, higher level of success. Mann wanted to create a school system that would make it possible for the children of immigrants from different countries to achieve the American dream. Much of this dream consisted of the promise that hard work and a good education would pay off in rising social and economic status. Creating a common school system would be the central path for children to advance. This is an argument for equity through education, which comes down to us in the phrase, "Every child can learn."

Eventually, many immigrants bought into this ideology and came to expect their children to acquire a good education in these terms. In the early years after the Industrial Revolution, Native Americans and people of color were locked out of the school system. The reality of successful school participation is still unevenly distributed across Americans. Many parents continue to hope that their children will attend one of the country's elite colleges, even though they themselves may never have finished high school or gone to college.

We think that the expectations for education are beginning to change once again. The goal of success for all is still widely present. However, as many schools struggle to create greater opportunities for all families, teens and adults are assuming more responsibility for their own lives and education. They often look beyond what school has to offer, choosing to pursue instead whatever interests them or what they think is necessary to advance their careers. They are less willing to accept what educators have decreed through curriculum standards.

Rather, in the spirit of customization, many are pursuing their own educational paths, learning what they think will be of value to them. Choice reigns in charter schools, rich curricular electives, and virtual schooling options. Homeschooling is parents' way of saying, "We think we should decide what our children should learn." The proliferation of distance education, learning centers, and technical certifications acts to expand the choices that people can make about what they will learn. In this light, the standards movement can be seen as a conservative check on rampant customization.

Anya Kamenetz's (2010) idea of DIY education that describes how learners assemble their own education experiences from across institutions and organizations. Of course, there is an important economic component of this ability to choose among alternatives. Many people who pick their own paths have already taken advantage of what their education systems have to offer and can afford to pursue interest-based learning on their own terms. When Greg Duncan and Richard Murnane (2011) surveyed research on the limits of schooling, they found that the market for well-to-do parents and learners to pursue new pathways toward learning is one of the leading causes of inequality in academic outcomes. As the lifelong learning era moves gradually toward a situation where people choose for themselves what kind of education to obtain, schools will remain a significant part of legitimate learning—but only a part.

CONTENT: FROM PRACTICAL SKILLS TO DISCIPLINARY KNOWLEDGE TO LEARNING HOW TO LEARN

As already stated, before the Industrial Revolution, the major purposes of educating most children were religious salvation and learning to do the work that they would perform as adults. The content of education focused on literacy and the skills and crafts of their parents or masters, if they were apprenticed to a trade. Where schools for common people existed, they focused on a few basic skills, such as reading, writing, and basic computation, which children would need to read the Bible and carry out tasks such as the buying and selling of goods. Few students in common schools attended for more than a year or two. However, they did learn much from helping their parents at work and doing chores around the house. Most children learned how to make a living from their parents, but when a child was apprenticed in a craft or trade, the master took on the role of a parent. The major portion of education, for the great majority of children, focused on the practical skills of making a living. A few elite schools taught the knowledge and skills expected for leadership, but access to these schools was limited severely by social class distinctions.

With the Industrial Revolution, the important goal of education in the United States became preparing children to live in American society. The schools stressed learning a common core of knowledge, particularly reading, writing and arithmetic, which children would need to function as intelligent citizens and workers. As schooling extended through high school, the curriculum added knowledge in the various disciplines that developed in the modern era. History, English, and civics were stressed, to prepare students to be good citizens. Courses in algebra and geometry were added, to prepare students for the many professions that required mathematical training, such as finance, engineering, and scientific professions. The Committee of Ten, which convened in the 1890s, decided that every high school student should study English, mathematics, Latin and Greek, history, science, and geography, reflecting the disciplines that colleges felt were important. Their recommendations largely determined the academic high school curriculum in the 20th century, although Latin and Greek were dropped in favor of modern languages.

It is impossible for schools to teach people all the knowledge that they might need as adults. Extending schooling for more and more years to accommodate growing demands for education is not a viable strategy. Therefore, learning how to learn and how to find useful resources is becoming the most important goal of education. Therefore, the focus is more on so-called soft skills, such as problem solving and communication in different media, on interpersonal skills in order to interact with people from different backgrounds, and on learning to find the information and resources needed for accomplishing tasks. These ideas were outlined in a report from the U.S. Department of Labor called the SCANS Commission (1991) report. It argued that to prepare people for work in the 21st century, they needed education in five areas that they called "core competencies":

- *Resources:* Identifying, organizing, planning, and allocating resources
- *Interpersonal:* Working with others
- *Information:* Acquiring and using information

- *Systems:* Understanding complex interrelationships
- *Technology:* Working with a variety of technologies

They argued that these new competencies should be built upon a foundation of basic skills, thinking skills, and interpersonal qualities, such as responsibility and integrity. Over time, these initial skills described in the SCANS Commission report have blossomed into a vibrant international discussion over 21st-century skills needed to succeed in today's world.

The transition from disciplinary knowledge to learning how to learn is felt acutely in the changing labor market. Experts in the labor market emphasize the impossibility of predicting what jobs will be popular in 5 years, much less 20 or 30 years from now. Just as information technology is overturning education, it is also creating havoc in employment futures. Computerized automation, for example, cut back much of the blue-collar labor market in the United States in the last decades of the 20th century. Now, advances in artificial intelligence and logistics endanger most routine jobs. Even truck driving is under siege. Over the last century, as jobs have been disappearing and the demand for flexibility and thinking has grown, people who can find work will have to keep learning new knowledge and skills throughout their lifetimes as their lives and jobs keep changing (Collins, 2017).

PEDAGOGY: FROM APPRENTICESHIP TO DIDACTICISM TO INTERACTION

The pedagogy of apprenticeship involves modeling, observation, coaching, and practice. The mentor shows how to do things and then watches the learner, gradually reducing their support as the learner gains experience. Apprenticeship was not simply the method of teaching trades and crafts. It was how children learned how to run a farm or shop, how to be a midwife, how to do chores around the house, and even how to read and write when these skills were taught at home. Apprenticeship grew out of the patterns of people teaching in one-on-one situations. Apprenticeship is very resource intensive since it requires a knowledgeable adult, and intense interaction, for every two or three learners. However, it is very efficient because almost everyone manages to learn, given such close supervision. In the family, older siblings often take on some of the teaching, and in the trades, a master might have a number of apprentices, the more experienced of which help teach the novices.

Apprenticeship was not a viable pedagogy for mass schooling. When the schools were flooded with students, they had to evolve a mass pedagogy that would work for a very high ratio of students to teachers. The pedagogy of industrial-era schooling involved small numbers of teachers lecturing to large numbers of children about knowledge and skills, directing the children to practice by answering questions or doing homework, and then testing to see if they had learned what was taught. Lecturing proved the most efficient pedagogy since the teachers would need no other resources than their knowledge and ability to engage through speaking. The progressive educators argued that children learn better by active engagement rather than listening to teachers, so new methods that engaged students were adopted over time. These included engaging children in answering questions, reciting things that they had learned, filling out worksheets, doing homework, and carrying out projects and discussions. The pedagogy of schooling has come a long way from the early years, when, as Larry Cuban (1984) describes, students were expected to recite in order all the bays along the East Coast of the United States. But the pedagogy of public schooling remains based on mass production, with limited quality control.

The pedagogy of the lifelong-learning era is evolving toward reliance on interaction. Sometimes this involves interacting with a rich technological environment, such as a tutoring system or a video game, and sometimes interacting with other people, by means of a virtual network. The pedagogy of computer tutors echoes the apprenticeship model in setting individualized tasks for learners and offering guidance and feedback as they work. This type of guided pedagogy extends beyond computer tutors. For example, discussion-board interest groups can provide specific, task-level advice about how to solve a video game puzzle, whether to make a fantasy baseball trade, or how much stock should be purchased to balance a portfolio. As another example, a distance-learning teacher might monitor how a group of students are progressing on a project that they have been assigned to carry out.

Computers can't replace the rich, nuanced benefits of one-to-one social interaction. But networks can provide some of the social interaction that is missing in the mass-production classroom. Virtual networks, such as fan fiction sites, provide access to learning communities that support the kinds of individualized interaction found in apprenticeship communities.

ASSESSMENT: FROM OBSERVATION TO TESTING
TO EMBEDDED ASSESSMENT

In the apprenticeship era, mentors carefully observed learners and corrected them as they went along, giving them tasks that they were ready for, and seeing if they completed them successfully. This cycle of close supervision and feedback helped students to learn from making mistakes. This cycle also allowed the mentors to understand the capabilities of learners and to anticipate many of the problems that the student may have with new situations. The mentor can ward off failure by giving tasks that have the right amount of challenge—not too easy, so that learners become bored, and not too difficult, so they fail. When learners do make mistakes, the mentor can go over what was done and try to identify what led to any mistake. Assessment in this context, then, does not involve getting a grade or failing a test. It simply means getting feedback as you work, receiving suggestions about how to improve, and trying again. The mentor comes away with a clear understanding of what each apprentice is capable of doing; the student comes away with an assessment of just what still needs to be learned.

In the schooling era, this resource-intensive process of observation, feedback, and trying again became too expensive for a mass market. Testing emerged as the means to determine whether students had acquired the skills and knowledge that were taught. As with apprenticeship, the teacher's role was to formatively observe the student in order to provide direct feedback on the progress of learning. But teachers often could not assess the cumulative effects of the curriculum over time with so many students, so general tests were developed to track whether students had learned enough to advance to the next level. In the late 20th century, testing began to be used to assess the quality of the school and the teachers as well as the progress of the student. Testing always involves some cutoff, so it brought with it the notions of passing and failing. This led to the ranking of students, and ultimately to a sense of failure among those who did not learn at the same rate as peers.

In the lifelong-learning era, as with apprenticeship, assessment begins again to converge around the interests and abilities of the learner. This is particularly true in computer-based learning environments. As discussed in Chapter 5, this kind of assessment takes two forms. First, assessment can occur in computer-adaptive learning systems as the learner progresses through tasks in order to provide ongoing support to determine whether the learner has accomplished the desired goals. This kind of assessment is more like that in apprenticeship settings, where the assessment is ongoing and tightly coupled to the learning. When students need help, the computer may provide hints or suggestions as to how to proceed. When students make a mistake, the computer might point out the error or guide them toward the correct answer.

Second, assessment can happen in a virtual affinity group, such as a fan fiction site or maker space. When participants begin to make products that can be judged by other members of the group, they receive feedback on the work's perceived value, as well as comments on how to improve their work. As participants in the affinity group, receiving feedback incurs a responsibility to provide feedback for others. In both cases, computers make it easier to customize assessment for individual learners in the ongoing learning process. Receiving this kind of customized, just-in-time feedback makes it easier to learn from mistakes. To the degree that assessment can provide the appropriate support, it can ensure that everyone succeeds and feels a sense of accomplishment.

LOCATION: FROM HOME TO SCHOOL TO ANYWHERE

In the apprenticeship era, most work was done locally. The ability to travel far from any farm, town, or village was prohibitively expensive for most people. As a result, apprenticeship focused on the work available in local households and domestic industries. Children learned to carry out adult tasks from parents or relatives at home. In towns and cities, children might be sent to school for a year or two, but the demands of maintaining the home or local industry typically would draw children into the workplace as soon as they were able to take on work. The main venues for education were the home and the farm or shop attached to it.

With the Industrial Revolution, many parents started moving to cities and working in factories. Initially, children also were expected to join in the adults' factory work and were assigned to jobs where being small was an advantage. Social reformers in the United States and the United Kingdom in the late 19th century reported horrifying stories of child labor abuse in factories, and they began to push for alternative settings for children just to be children. Just as the child abuse stories were capturing the public attention, the push for universal schooling seemed to provide a solution for what to do with children who were no longer working on farms or in factories.

Reformers worked with civic leaders to create schools for children to learn the knowledge and skills to be citizens of a new urban and industrial culture. Gradually, school came to be seen as the major venue where education happened. Soon other institutions began to adopt the school model as a place for organized learning. Hospitals, workplaces, the military, and businesses created school like settings when they wanted to train people to do tasks. Not only did these institutions adopt the idea of school, they also adopted the techniques of mass pedagogy that came along with it. Norman Frederiksen (1984) told the story of how he was assigned to improve the assessment of gunner's mates for the U.S. Navy during World War II. This is a job that requires cleaning and maintaining guns onboard ships, but he found that the teaching was by lecture and the testing done with pencil and paper. He proposed to institute a performance test based on the tasks that gunner's mates actually carry out. The instructors objected to this because they thought that the students would fail. Just as the instructors predicted, the learners all failed the performance test, but Frederiksen insisted that the new test be kept. After they failed, students demanded to be taught how to do the tasks on which they would be tested. Soon they learned to do just as well on the performance test as they had previously done on the pencil-and-paper test. This story illustrates how as schooling became the dominant metaphor for organized learning, it led to ineffective ways to teach practical skills.

Now education is moving into many different venues, where learning materials can be accessed from computers and the web. In-person interpersonal interaction continues to have significant value in all forms of learning, and it likely will never be replaced completely by virtual learning. Still, the ability to access learning environments online is greatly expanding the concept of where education takes place. Lifelong learners often use new media technologies, such as smart phones, to access their learning environments and communities. Many towns and buildings are providing wireless connections, and this connectivity is spreading rapidly. We are approaching the era when people can engage in just-in-time learning anytime and anywhere.

CULTURE: FROM ADULT CULTURE TO PEER CULTURE
TO MIXED-AGE CULTURE

Before the Industrial Revolution, adults defined culture. Children were seen (if they were seen at all) as little adults who needed to learn the culture of the adults in their community. While they might form close bonds with their brothers and sisters or fellow apprentices, their work was serious business, and learning to do the work was crucial to their own and their family's survival. The notion that there was a separate youth culture, or even adolescence as a developmental category, did not emerge in the apprenticeship era. What youth culture there was largely reflected the activities and experiences that adults thought would be appropriate for youth.

As James Coleman (1961) pointed out, a separate youth peer culture arose with the advent of Industrial Age schooling. This new peer culture reflected the opinions of adolescents and, as the 20th century progressed, often ran counter to the expectations and values of adult culture. Middle schools and high schools concentrated same-aged children together, which led to the development of peer culture. Kids have to be old enough and concentrated enough to form a community with its own beliefs and values. When peer culture developed, it began to reflect the newly recognized interests and needs of adolescents.

In the 1980s, Penelope Eckert (1989) described how peer culture in a typical American high school developed between two poles: the jock culture and the burnout culture. The jocks consisted of all the students who fully participated in school activities and played by the school rules. The burnouts were the students who were hostile to the school and teachers, often doing drugs or other non-school activities. While Eckert found that most students fell in between these two groups, the two formed the axis around which the school culture revolved. Adolescent peer culture has transformed the entertainment, fashion, and advertising industries, and has become a distracting contender for the attention of youth who do not find a place for themselves in the culture of schools.

As education becomes more linked to interest-based online cultures that include members with different levels of expertise and different age levels, learning is likely to be less influenced by the effects of local peer culture. Mimi Ito et al. (2010) developed categories of hanging out, messing around, and geeking out, as discussed in Chapter 5, which represent another way to think about the diversity of culture with new media. In Ito's terms, the transition from hanging out to messing around is likely to create more situations where people of different ages are learning together. This will tend to create a new kind of mixed-age learning culture.

RELATIONSHIPS: FROM PERSONAL BONDS TO AUTHORITY FIGURES TO COMPUTER-MEDIATED INTERACTION

In the apprenticeship era, children were learning from the adults in their local environment. Most education came from their parents or close relatives and friends. Children typically formed close bonds with the people who were teaching them. The closeness of the bonds had many significant effects on their learning. Children knew that if they did not try hard, they would disappoint people who were critical to their survival. In times of poverty and limited opportunity, a child's failure to learn through apprenticeship had real consequences for families. Hence, most children learned what they could in order to satisfy the adults who were teaching them.

With the advent of universal schooling, children and teachers must build their relationships anew at the start of each school year. Given that they are strangers at the outset, many-to-one student-teacher ratios make it difficult to build the same kinds of relationships seen in apprenticeship. The ability to establish enduring learning relationships with students usually depends on whether the teacher demonstrates the authority to control the classroom. In most middle and high schools, teachers must establish their authority from the outset or they will not survive very long. It is the students who perceive the value of schooling to their futures who are most likely to recognize the authority of the teacher role as a necessary stepping stone to make schooling work. When students don't recognize the authority of the teacher or the school, the classroom becomes rife with conflict. There is a clear power relationship between the giving and receiving of authority in school.

Lifelong learning restores some of the relationship characteristics of apprenticeship learning. When students participate in web communities or take distance education courses, they interact with teachers and other students over the Internet based on common interests. These kinds of virtual interactions are not as rich as apprenticeships, but they often are richer than the limited contact that students have with teachers at school.

Computer-based learning environments affect the learning relationship in another way: computer systems have limited under-standing of students as individuals and do not provide the warmth and support of a good human teacher. At the same time, the systems provide regular, targeted feedback in a noncritical, impartial manner. Much is lost in computer-based learning settings because we learn most naturally by interacting with people whom we know well and respect. But the highly interactive nature of computer environments may compensate in part for the lack of personal bonds. Given the limitations of computer environments, it is best if students working in computer-mediated environments are part of a community, either offline with friends and family or online with people sharing common interests.

CRITICAL TRANSFORMATIONS IN EDUCATION

Perhaps the most striking change from the era of apprenticeship to the era of universal schooling was the state's assumption of responsibility for educating children. State control of education led to a mass-schooling model that aggregated students into age groups, promoted standardized curricula and assessment methods, and reconfigured the relationship between teachers and learners. We think that in the lifelong-learning era, people interested in advancing their own learning will begin to take back responsibility for education from the state. At the same time, though, learners who are unwilling or unable to take advantage of the possibilities that the new technologies offer for lifelong learning are likely to suffer.

CHAPTER 7

What May Be Lost and What May Be Gained

New information technologies alter learning everywhere. As we have seen, the tremors have shaken the world of education, schooling, and learning to the core. As with any revolution, there will be gains and losses. A dystopian view sees people becoming subservient to their technologies and many people being left behind as technology comes to dominate their lives. From this perspective, technologies gang up to push aside people's abilities to think deeply (Carr, 2011), institutions become weak and unable to fulfill their social promises, and people increasingly lose agency over their lives. Utopians foresee a golden age of learning opening before us, in which people will be able to find the resources to pursue any education they want. Futures are rarely predicted by either optimistic or pessimistic forecasts. Part of each vision will come to pass, as well as effects that we cannot hope to anticipate. In this chapter, we consider some of the fears and the hopes present in the current tensions between schooling and technology.

WHAT MAY BE LOST

In Thomas Jefferson's and Horace Mann's visions, public education would prepare people to be good citizens and assimilate them to a common culture. Mann was very concerned about how democracies would induct immigrants into American society so they would develop a common sense of citizenship and social cohesion. In the 20th century, public schooling became a favorite vehicle to address Mann's concerns. A public schooling system that would accept all children, from all families, into programs that would correct the disadvantages of social class and allow access to opportunity for all learners was the original dream of education reformers. This vision of a possible future for public schooling continues to inspire generations of educators, researchers, reformers, and policymakers. Despite the recurrent failures to realize this dream fully, education, more than any other institution, carries the dreams of building a society that improves on the errors and inequities of prior generations.

The promise of education depends on the identification of schooling with learning. If we place our hopes in improving schooling as the key pathway to a better life, then we can, ideally, maintain some control over our ability to progress toward a brighter future. Private and religious schools, charter schools, and homeschooling have eroded the ability to focus social attention on a single point of contact for improving education. The advent of interest-based, technology-driven media has dramatically fragmented the identification of schooling with education.

Interest-based education fragments the current system by creating alternative pathways to achieve the outcomes of the current education system. New technologies invite parents and individuals to assume the responsibility for learning core subjects like math, science, and reading. For example, parents can enlist private tutors or enroll in learning centers to supplement the instruction their children received in school. In Ontario, Canada, about 24% of parents with school-aged children have hired tutors, and 50% claim that they would hire tutors if they could afford them (Davies & Aurini, 2006). Students can also use Khan Academy or sign up for courses on EdX or Open University to develop alternative learning certifications. Tutoring, learning centers, and online courses amplify the learning for their participants. However, when students who are able to participate in these supplemental programs compete against students who are limited to the resources provided by school, this creates an alternative path to learning that undermines the power of the school to provide an equitable learning environment for all students.

The more radical version of alternative pathways is for parents and learners to opt out of state-run schools entirely. This has been available to families who could afford tuition or who could teach their children at home, of course. New technologies strengthen alternative programs by creating access to higher-quality learning tools. Choosing to opt out of the public system results in fracturing education into smaller, interest-based groups. Families who can afford to do so splinter off into schools that support their religious or political viewpoints, developing curricula that address the concerns they have about raising children. As David Brooks (2004) argues, we are settling into our own "cultural zones," where like-minded people cluster together.

By such fracturing into interest groups, citizenship and social cohesion goals are likely to be undermined. When the American republic was new, there was a general concern about whether it could hold together as a single union, given how diverse the peoples and their values were in the individual states. These differences came to a head in the Civil War. The ongoing struggle to create union in the midst of a diverse, immigrant nation continued through the 20th century. By the 1950s, centralized control over commercial and public media had created a monocultural façade that gave the appearance of universal culture and support for public institutions. During the 1960s and 1970s, however, the monoculture began to fracture through the rise of teen culture and the civil rights movement. Schooling continued to be celebrated as a public pathway toward opportunity for all, but the eroded sense of common culture resulted in an enhanced consumer ethic, where each person was expected to choose according to his or her own interests. The celebration of interest and choice has eroded a shared commitment to public schooling as well.

The technological turn in contemporary schooling itself has led to unanticipated consequences. In the 1990s and 2000s, scholars and policymakers were concerned with the digital divide—the difference in access to computers and the web between rich and poor. Schools have been the means by which many immigrants and minorities gained access to the American mainstream. As Larry Cuban (2001, 2013) has documented, efforts to include computers in schools have been thwarted by the dominance of existing practices of teaching and learning. If students couldn't afford new technologies at home and couldn't access them in schools either, then poor students were deprived of the advantages of new technologies for learning.

The situation has changed in the 2010s. Now that most people access virtual resources through mobile devices, tablets, and gaming systems, the gap between the rich and poor for online access is shrinking (Anderson, 2017). However, the new digital divide takes the form of what Henry Jenkins and his colleagues (2007) call the "participation gap." Learners from families where virtual resources are included in everyday interaction are picked up by children as key components of self-designed learning environments. It rarely occurs to children for whom technologies are used only for entertainment or social interactions to use applications such as YouTube or Google to help with homework. When schools neglect to include virtual learning resources and the devices that support these tools in everyday practices of teaching, then the inequities in the knowledge and skills brought by students to their classrooms goes unchallenged.

Despite widespread tracking, segregation, and market fragmentation, the public schools are the institution that fosters equity more than any other institution in America. As Martin Carnoy and Henry Levin (1985, p. 2) argue, "Schooling produces relatively more equal outcomes than the workplace and other institutions of the larger society." Families who choose to take their resources outside the local school system to support their children's learning weaken the capacity of schools to create better opportunities for all families. Diminishing the resources of the system makes it likely that poor children will have fewer chances to interact with the kinds of resources and peer interactions that lead to new opportunities. The danger is that public schools may be left with the students who have no other choice, while parents who can provide other resources will avail themselves of environments that take full advantage of new technologies for learning.

Education has long been perceived by parents as critical to getting ahead. This reflects the growing disparity in income between college-educated and noncollege-educated people (Murnane & Levy, 1996). Even though schools have instituted policies to help some students get ahead, such as gifted and talented programs, Advanced Placement (AP) courses, and tracking, public schools were conceived to be egalitarian institutions. Hence, parents are spending more money to buy their children educational services, such as educational videos and games, computer-based resources, private schooling, and specialized tutoring, so that their children will have an advantage. Poor families can't afford many of these services and may not even be aware that they exist, which exacerbates the educational inequalities that public schools have tried to mitigate.

New media technologies, as described in Chapter 5, are also destabilizing the employment market. The resulting uncertainty of the work world has led many policymakers, parents, and learners to embrace supposedly safer education pathways into the workforce, such as computer science, business, medicine, and communications. In an uncertain employment market, will children be steered along narrow paths that their parents approve of, such as a particular religious or job orientation? This may lead to people growing more insular and finding it difficult to get along with people from different backgrounds or with different views. Further, children may not be open to considering a wide range of occupations because their parents may try to limit their choices, as was done in societies before the spread of schooling. Mann's conception of public schooling was to build an institution that would foster a more tolerant society, where people encounter many different ideas and types of people. Will this all be cut short by the Balkanization of education?

Finally, will the dominance of virtual interaction for learning result in people becoming more isolated and interacting less with other people socially? It is by interacting with supportive mentors and teachers that people are inspired to work hard and learn difficult topics. Isolation could produce a loss of social skills and societal cohesion. Traditionally, school has been a place where children learned to trust and work with others. The effect of virtual tools on social cohesion is a lively area of study. Sherry Turkle (2015) wonders how interaction with virtual devices is damaging our children's abilities to converse. Nicholas Carr (2011) claims that the distractions of the new technologies are eroding our abilities to concentrate on longer, more sophisticated arguments. Jaron Lanier (2011) raises the existential question of who we are when we have established digital identities in virtual worlds beyond our control. The decline in trust and in the number of people participating in community organizations has already been well documented by Robert Putnam (2000). We worry that the technologizing of education will further the decline in community among Americans, at the same time that the population is becoming more diverse.

Many of these problems are exacerbated by the privatization trend that took hold during the 1980s. There has been an increasing inclination worldwide, but particularly in the United States, to encourage people to become consumers in all kinds of markets. While this allows savvy people to make more of their own choices and purchase their own educational resources, it leaves less educated or affluent people further behind in the competition for educational resources. The move toward thinking of education as a market with consumers has the effect of increasing educational disparities for most communities. Technology so far has been a force for increasing rather than decreasing inequality.

To summarize the pessimistic view of the future, we see technology as a market-driven pressure to increase inequality and to fragment the public commitment to schooling. The elites commit more resources in order to give their children an edge in the education race. They buy games, devices, and programs for their children when they are preschoolers. They send them to expensive preschools. They buy them computers at an early age, so they can learn to navigate the web and acquire critical technology skills. They send them to private schools or buy houses in neighborhoods with elite public schools. They contribute time and resources to their children's schools, so they will be able to provide the kids with the best possible schooling. They get their kids tutoring if they are having trouble with any of their classes. They send them to take Scholastic Aptitude Test (SAT) and American College Testing (ACT) prep courses at a local learning center. Elites can and do buy kids the best possible education so that they can beat the competition in later life.

State courts have tried to restore equity by mandating that states distribute resources more fairly among their towns and cities. But many elites in the states resist such redistribution of resources with all their might. In an extreme example, one rich county in Vermont, facing a mandate to redistribute finances to poorer counties in the state, actually tried to secede from Vermont and join New Hampshire across the river. It is going to be very difficult to reallocate resources more fairly among schools across the country, and the availability now of vast technological resources only exacerbates the problem. To redress the problem will take a much broader vision of education than educators now have.

WHAT MAY BE GAINED

One of the most powerful promises offered by technology is that learning will become more engaging. Education will be directed more toward what people want to learn, and hence they will be more excited and drawn to learning. For example, parents who are schooling their children at home usually encourage them to pursue topics in which they are interested more deeply than other topics. They try to embed important learning goals, such as math and writing, into those contexts, so that the children devote themselves to doing a good job. Furthermore, when people choose courses in distance education or adult education, they choose topics that they feel will help their careers or that reflect their abiding interests. And, of course, when people watch and produce videos on YouTube, play multiplayer games, or engage in crowdsourced learning communities, they become members of learning communities whose work they value. The shift from passive to active learning, facilitated by new media technologies, can have a profound effect on engagement.

Despite its effect on increasing inequity, commercialization of education also may act to increase students' engagement in learning. Products developed by commercial firms, whether courses, videos, or software, will be designed to attract buyers and consumers. Khan Academy, TenMarks, and YouTube thrive best when more people engage and produce on their sites. The revenue stream from new media technologies is increasingly shifting from direct consumer payment for products and services to advertising revenues generated by the number of participants that the site can produce. Sites like Wikipedia and Reddit are mostly cost-free for participants, thus greatly expanding the economic range of possible users.

The new media education market is clearly growing rapidly, and many firms are entering it, such as Google and Amazon. They are developing new approaches to education that clearly appeal to people. As the monopoly of the district school comes undone, it will free educational institutions and products to compete for students. But the question remains: Who will be buying, and how?

Another potential gain stems from the capability of computer-adaptive learning tools to customize education to the particular needs and abilities of learners. Computer learning environments can be designed to provide hints and support to students when they need help. This support can be allocated carefully, so that students get as much help as they need, but not too much. This allows learners to tackle tasks that they might not otherwise be able to attempt, and to succeed when they do. Hence, learners can be given tasks that are challenging to them, in which they learn a lot and feel a sense of accomplishment upon completion. In this way, computer environments can adapt to the level of each student's ability and help all students to succeed.

Technology also can make it possible to access knowledge anytime, anywhere through the web. Universal access to learning would have profound effects. If people are at home with an Internet connection, in the future, they may have all the world's knowledge at their fingertips—not just in the form of text, but in videos, tutorials, and simulations. In an ideal world, universal access may even be provided to poor people around the world. The 1:1 computer-to-children ratio is becoming increasingly common in U.S. schools. As this investment makes 1:1

a feasible goal, we may eventually see a tipping point, at which the pervasiveness of the technology redefines teaching and learning.

As education becomes more tailored to people's interests and abilities, the competition between students in school may diminish. In the apprenticeship era, Jean Lave (1988) argues that almost everyone successfully learned the skills that they were taught. One of the fundamental problems of school is that children are always comparing themselves to other students, and only the best students feel that they are successful. Because school is so competitive, a sense of failure overwhelms many students. Many students turn to extracurricular activities, become disengaged, or simply drop out. Even for successful students, the goal of getting grades fails to spark a real love of learning. In an interest-driven, technology-rich environment, learners are more likely to find their own way in communities organized around shared interests, so that failure experienced as part of learning can be seen as a step toward belonging in a wider community of practice.

If people are learning at work or at home in virtual learning environments, they will succeed only if they take responsibility for their own learning. When the state took over responsibility for teaching children, families and individuals ceded most of the responsibility to the schools. Many schoolchildren seem to defy the schools to teach them anything. But people are not going to learn much unless they take responsibility for their own learning. Teachers struggle to inspire their charges to take responsibility for their learning, and many succeed, but many others fail. Technology may create interest-driven spaces that help put students in charge of their own learning.

REALIZING THE PROMISE AND MITIGATING THE DANGER

Our hope is that as more children and adults become aware of how critical education is to success, more and more segments of society will avail themselves of the new opportunities that these technology-based resources make possible. We also see technology becoming cheaper and more technology-based resources becoming freely available. The exciting part of the information technology revolution is how many new resources are available for free to anyone who can get online. Most people will be able to participate in the academic-based or interest-based educational activities that they desire at any time, at their own pace.

Whether the potential losses outweigh the potential gains of the emerging education system remains a matter for debate. How society acts to take advantage of the promise and mitigate the dangers is an issue of immediate concern. Technology holds the promise of engaging students in deep learning and pushing students to become the best-educated people they can be. We as a society should think about how to make that promise come to fruition. How can the schools tap into the technology revolution most effectively? And how can we capitalize on the technology resources outside the schools?

CHAPTER 8

How Schools Can Support the New Technologies

We are in the midst of a great opportunity to redefine the relation of education and schooling. New media technologies are creating new pathways to traditional academic goals, as well as forging virtual communities of production and exchange for interest-based learning. This is a time of opportunity for educators—one that we have not faced in more than 150 years. To be effective, the stakeholders who are working to build a new education system must understand the imperatives of the technologies that are driving this revolution.

We have encapsulated those imperatives in terms of customization, interaction, and learner control. *Customization* refers to providing people the knowledge that they want, when they want it, and supporting and guiding people individually as they learn. *Interaction* refers to the ability of computers to give learners immediate feedback and to engage learners actively in accomplishing realistic tasks. *Learner control* refers to putting learners in charge of their own learning whenever possible, so they feel ownership and can direct their learning wherever their interests take them.

Change in U.S. public education is popularly understood as a pendulum swinging between local, community control and centralized, national control of schools. In the 1990s and early 2000s, the pendulum appeared to be swinging away from local control and toward nationally defined standards and standardized testing. In an effort to provide equality of outcomes, federal and state policies have emphasized accountability by promoting standardized educational testing and pressuring schools to adopt uniform practices in classrooms. Particularly in urban areas, this emphasis on accountability is providing mixed results. The new accountability policies have made some headway in improving student achievement across the country, as measured by standardized tests (Hanushek & Raymond,

2005). Still, high-stakes testing runs the risk of encouraging educators to "game" the system, producing reportable results without significant improvement to student learning (Amrein & Berliner, 2002; Jones, Jones, & Hargrove, 2003).

As a side effect of accountability policies, schools have expanded their technology infrastructure greatly. Nearly 100% of U.S. public schools have adopted sophisticated data analysis and student information system tools, and the majority of schools have adopted some form of learning management system. By 2010, 99% of U.S. public school districts had student information systems, 77% had data warehouses, and 64% had curriculum management systems (Means, Padilla, & Gallagher, 2010). By 2014, the global market for management and information technologies had swelled to a $1 billon industry (Herold, 2014). During the 2000s, schools also began to invest in computer-adaptive assessment tools that would use computer-adaptive testing technologies to provide instant, standards-based feedback on student learning (Burch, 2010). These investments in technology were driven by the need to address standards-based accountability policies. The resulting technological capacity to address information needs brought school leaders and administrators into the 21st century.

Now the political pendulum is swinging back toward local, community control of schools. The Common Core State Standards Initiative started with great momentum in 2009 as a cumulative effort to define consistently what counts as quality learning in math and literacy for all schools and all learners. In coordination with the U.S. Department of Education's Race to the Top Initiative, the Common Core was to determine what counts as good teaching and learning in the United States. But in the mid-2010s, critics from the political right and left claimed that the push for national standards and accountability were undercutting the role that parents, communities, and even students should play in defining educational programs and outcomes. As of 2017, the future of Common Core and the centralized control of U.S. education and accountability policies are in peril as both local and national leaders debate what comes next.

This swing toward national control over schooling runs against the grain of the technological imperatives of customization, interaction, and learner control. To cope with these imperatives, schools need to embrace technologies that embody more individual support and choice in how and what students learn. They will need to use the tools that invite students to participate in more challenging and realistic tasks that reflect the uses of knowledge in the world. The activities will need to be more individualized and interest-based than current school activities. The tasks will need to make sense to students and need to be more oriented to the students' long-term goals and interests. These imperatives have strong implications for the design of curriculum, assessment, and equity.

Here, we propose several areas for policy development to help public schools take advantage of new media. Hopefully, initiatives in these directions will help public schools to participate in, rather than to resist, the ongoing educational revolution. We do not need to start a new education system from scratch. Designing a better education system means understanding where the existing pieces can best be reshaped, brought together, or played down. In this chapter, we discuss three areas that might help bring together the best of the old and the new: performance-based assessment, new curriculum designs, and new approaches to equity in a digital world.

PERFORMANCE-BASED ASSESSMENT

The national obsession with standardized testing has led some researchers to pursue new understandings of how to measure learning. We would like to highlight two aspects of this recent work: national certifications and skill-based assessment systems.

One way to bring together established and new approaches to learning would be to develop a set of national credentials that could be administered on computer or by trained professionals at any school or learning center. People would be able to apply for as many credential certifications, or badges, as they like and take the exams for them whenever they feel they are ready. This differs from school, where exams are administered when the teacher or district decide. These credentials would be much more narrowly focused than a high school diploma. Instead of institutional certifications, as with diplomas or degrees, these credentials would certify a learner's expertise with respect to specific skills.

By tying badges to the specific goals of learners and their parents, assessment could be much more attuned to the technological imperatives of customization and learner control. If a student's goal is to become a doctor, she might need to get certificates to demonstrate expertise in chemistry, biology, psychology, and college-level literacy and math skills, etc. If he wants to become a travel agent, he will need to establish expertise in reading, listening, explaining, geography, psychology, resource management, scheduling, etc. There would need to be an online system that parents and students could consult to learn what certificates are needed for different career choices, what students need to know to obtain each certificate, and what methods they might use to obtain the necessary knowledge.

We see the certifications as being developed in three areas: academic skills, generic skills, and technical skills. In the academic area, there might be an English competency certificate at different grade levels of reading and writing competency and certification exams in history, math, languages, science, the arts, and other school disciplines. Getting a certain badge would allow students to move on to the next level of schooling, as with the current diploma system. If people wanted to take courses to prepare for the exams, they could; or if they wanted to study on their own, they could. Some people might obtain a large number of these credentials, and some might obtain fewer credentials.

The generic skills' certifications would follow the general guidelines of the Department of Labor's SCANS Commission (1991) report, which suggests five competency areas: resource allocation, working with others, acquiring and using information, understanding complex systems, and working with a variety of technologies. Within each area, there might be a number of different credentials. Technical skills would be focused on specific skills required for the workplace, such as automotive diagnosis, coding, and network administration. Students would choose which certificates they want to earn, and they would know in advance how their performance in carrying out assessment tasks would be judged.

The choice of credentials that they try for would be up to the students and their parents and would depend on their career interests and plans. Of course, one problem with a badging system would be for students who do not know yet exactly which educational path to take. In this new educational world, most children would continue with the kinds of elementary schools and middle schools that they now attend, to make sure that they had experience with different kinds of students and teachers and could envision different educational paths. The internal organization of these schools, however, would be organized around credentialing requirements rather than specific courses based on Carnegie units. At the next level, students would continue to take a series of required credentialing programs, but also would have increasing autonomy to select their preferred credentials. To help them make these decisions, they should have access to a multimedia advisory system to learn about the sorts of credentials that are valued by employers in different job categories, businesses, and professions.

So far, this design sounds like the current high-school-requirement-and-electives design, except that students, rather than teachers, would decide when they are ready to take an exam. Everything would depend upon the integrity of the certification system for credentialing. Ensuring the integrity of the certification system would require content experts to agree on what is worth knowing. The certification standard process would build on the already-robust subject-matter-standards discussions of the National Council of Teachers of Mathematics or the Advanced Placement (AP) programs. The conversations about what is worth knowing, and certifying, could draw out areas of agreement between school- and technology-based teachers and point to how the national standards movement could describe what students actually need to know and do as a result of their educational experiences.

Computers are revolutionizing how we measure what people know. As discussed in Chapter 5, computer-adaptive learning systems use a test-taker's prior answers to select which items best measure what the student knows. If a student fails to answer a question, the system provides an easier question; if successful, the student receives a more difficult question. Currently used for exams such as the Graduate Record Exam (GRE) and the Test of English as a Foreign Language (TOEFL), computer-adaptive testing technologies open up a range of assessment uses that could link old and new approaches to schooling and learning.

Computer-based testing also will help to capture the kinds of knowledge and skills required for learning in the professions. These assessments allow researchers to specify and measure the kinds of professional knowledge that previously had been observable only through performance. Mislevy, Steinberg, Breyer, and Almond (2002), a study of evidence-centered assessment, shows how assessments can be designed around sophisticated models of expert knowledge and can be used to measure what professionals such as dental hygienists need to know and do. These evidence-based assessments link the knowledge to be assessed, the behaviors that demonstrate knowledge, and the tasks that elicit the behaviors into a computer-adaptive testing system. The underlying knowledge models from such assessment systems are complex and difficult to construct, but they point to how measures of the skills and knowledge developed in K–12 schooling can be extended to capture professional knowledge.

Evidence-centered assessments also can be used with certification systems to focus educational discussion on the outcomes of learning. Assessment activities, then, could be more like authentic tasks developed by knowledgeable members of the educational, business, and assessment communities. Students could attempt to earn credentials as many times as they would like, and the evaluators in the assessment centers would have the responsibility of helping students understand the strengths and weaknesses of their performance and how they might improve in their next attempt at earning the credential. Earning a credential would provide students with an opportunity to have their accomplishments recognized by knowledgeable professionals and evaluated according to standards that are accepted by these professionals' community.

Students would create a portfolio of credentials for the purpose of employment or submitting college applications. Unlike current high school and college diploma certifications, the performance-based certification system would be linked to the kinds of knowledge and skills that mattered for adult learning. Developing a performance-based certification system also would force educators to be more careful about defining what they expect students to know and do.

NEW CURRICULUM DESIGNS

New media technologies open new avenues for curriculum development, ranging from new forms of teaching and learning to new ways of organizing how students and teachers interact. One curriculum design that we favor is using technology to help students focus their learning around their goals and interests. Such schools would place students in curricula based on their goals and interests, rather than on their ages or on the prevailing curriculum of their schools (for a more extended description, see Collins, 2017).

As discussed in Chapter 5, maker spaces and youth media arts organizations provide a model for how these programs might look in schools. A curriculum might start off in the early years with topics of interest to young children, such as families, pets, sports, or dinosaurs, and progress to areas such as filmmaking and media production, bio-medicine, or business management. Traditional academic skills, such as reading, writing, mathematics, science, history, and geography, would be woven into each curriculum. Students would pursue investigations and projects around issues they care about.

Students would be encouraged to stick with a particular curriculum for a long time—perhaps several years—while they develop deep skills and understanding. Each child, with the help of parents, would choose two curricula to start with, but might change from one curriculum to another, with the agreement of the teachers and parents. As children advance, they would move into curricula that reflect the kinds of things that adults do in the world, such as learning about the arts, business, or technology. But they should not change curricula frequently, or else they will never develop deep skills and knowledge in any domain.

Such a curriculum emphasizes students learning important content and skills in the context of carrying out complex tasks, such as making a video about the evolution of dinosaurs. A four-stage model for student learning in this kind of curriculum reflects how learning could be structured:

1. Students come in as novices and work on a small project of their own, with one of the more experienced students mentoring them as they carry out the project.
2. As they gain experience, they begin to work on larger projects with other students, where more advanced students serve as project and subproject leaders.
3. After they have worked on a number of different projects, they are ready to serve as a mentor for a new student.
4. After they successfully mentor new students, they are ready to begin serving as a project or subproject leader on larger projects.

When students become teenagers, we would trust them to follow a number of different paths. They might attend school, work, study at home to take certificate exams, or participate in organizations like YouthRadio, Digital Youth Network, or Maker Corps. If they want to go to college, they might try to get all the certifications that they need for college as soon as possible. Hence, some might go off to college at age 15 or 16. Others might work for a while and then come back to school to prepare for college. Ideally, the state would pay for a student's education to prepare for a certain number of certificates (perhaps 20 or 30). Then people could take courses whenever they are ready, at whatever age. Developing policies that encourage mixed-age population in courses, filled with people who have chosen to be there, might well alleviate some of the current problems with motivating students to participate in high school.

David Shaffer (2004, 2006) offers an alternative design to organize schooling around professional practices. Shaffer argues that school curricula are currently organized around antiquated forms of thought that make it difficult for students to link what they learn to what they will do later in life. Professions such as journalism, urban planning, and engineering have organized knowledge, beliefs, values, and strategies into what Shaffer calls *epistemic frames*. These frames have been refined over time and offer well-honed models for integrating knowing and doing. Game-based learning technologies can play a key role in introducing students to epistemic frames.

In the urban planning curriculum, for example, Shaffer developed an interactive tool that allows students to represent and manipulate buildings, parks, sanitation, and parking space. The tool is grounded in the real practices of urban planners and embedded in a curriculum designed to help students make predictions, experiment with their solutions, and face political heat for their decisions. Together, the tool and the curriculum provide an excellent introduction to the political, financial, and architectural dimensions of urban planning. Using established professions as the basis for curriculum design allows Shaffer to explore how students can learn math, history, science, and politics connected to authentic contexts.

Other approaches to fitting learning technologies into schools could focus on the topics that schools have typically had difficulty teaching, such as scientific investigation or historical and ecological systems. Citizen science, for example, draws learners into authentic science practices as data gatherers or to recognize patterns in data. Professional scientists then interpret the data and make models to describe, for example, population migrations or star constellations. Video games also can provide learners with experiences that schools find it difficult to re-create. Games such as *Civilization* build on models of historical progress and conflict, allowing players to see how cultures that develop religious, military, economic, or cultural superiority can influence the course of world development. After playing such games, students should reflect in groups on the historical implications of the events as they unfolded. In particular, they should try to relate what happened to events that they have read about in books and seen in videos of historical events, such as World War II. This glimpse into the process of how history unfolds is lacking in most textbook-dominated, fact-based approaches to history learning in schools. System-modeling games like *Civilization* and *SimCity* could help students gain new experiences to motivate learning critical knowledge and skills.

Outside the realm of standards-based subject matter, games can help students develop interpersonal and leadership skills. Massively multiplayer online games (MMOGs), such as *World of Warcraft*, allow players to solve complex problems involving strategy, logistics, and resource allocation. In MMOGs, players interact with social groups to recruit and retain new members, coordinate large-scale movements, and make decisions about political values. Such games give players a chance to develop strategic and leadership skills, leading John Seely Brown and Doug Thomas (2006) to suggest that video games may well be the environments that train the next generation of business leaders.

A final point about how technologies could affect schooling concerns course management systems. Many colleges and universities use systems from companies such as Canvas and Moodle for online access to discussion boards, collaborative project development spaces, and online textbooks and readings. While these systems typically organize content developed by teachers and publishers, the communication tools provided can open up spaces for more engaged learning. Students can use discussion boards, for example, to explore some of the difficult readings or to engage students in group design for course projects. More important, students who find it difficult to participate in class discussions can use online discussions to interact with and get to know their classmates. Course management systems integrate the kinds of communication technologies used outside of school into typical course content. Although K–12 schools have been slow to adopt course management tools, K–12 students accustomed to texting and SnapChat will quickly recognize how course management systems can open up new opportunities for interaction. Using course management systems for basic K–12 courses will help integrate communication technologies into the core of existing school programs.

NEW APPROACHES TO EQUITY IN A DIGITAL WORLD

Schools must face the challenge of harnessing the power of new media tools even as the pendulum of innovation is swinging toward technology products marketed to families with means. Technology-based learning venues allow families with means to supplement or to opt out of the public system in order to support their children's education. As a result, it appears that new media learning technologies mostly increase the inequity of opportunity. How can learning technologies be used to address the systemic inequities of public schools?

We feel that, in addition to the curricular ideas described in this chapter, new media open access to new kinds of educational experiences and affinity groups. Writers such as Jonathan Kozol (2005) paint a bleak picture of how many urban students, despite living in thriving cities, rarely travel out of their own neighborhoods and become trapped by the impoverished academic fare that dominates their classrooms. Virtual communities are very well suited to serve the needs of learners who are unable to travel. YouTube communities, for example, invite users to peruse an extraordinary variety of videos from anywhere. Learners can virtually connect with these diverse communities in many ways. Place-based video games, such as *ARIS* (fieldday. aris.org), can put learners in a position to virtually experience faraway spaces. Fan fiction sites can encourage students to write about faraway places and get feedback from authors around the world on aspects of their writing. James Paul Gee's (2013) concept of affinity spaces invites participants in virtual environments to learn how people around the world think, act, speak, and argue about new issues and topics. Learning technologies may not be able to address the underlying economic limits faced by students unable to travel outside their homes, but they can bring high-quality experiences and access to widespread communities into local schools.

New media technologies can also create opportunities to experience high-quality academic programs. The College Board's Advanced Placement (AP) program, for example, has proven one of the few educational innovations to successfully "go to scale." High school students from around the country take AP courses in literature, the social and natural sciences, mathematics, and other subjects that are graded on a common scale by external evaluators to ensure common outcomes. Still, it is difficult for many schools to offer a wide range of AP classes because of staff commitments and lack of student interest. The drastic cost reduction of video teleconferencing makes shared access to AP courses through distance education a ready option for many poor urban and rural schools. Organizations such as the Florida Virtual School increasingly act as brokers for providing courses that local schools are unable to offer (see, e.g., American Youth Policy Forum, 2002).

Virtual tutoring is another example of how technology can add to a school's academic resources. Tutoring is a favorite option for families with means to accelerate academic achievement. In the 2000s, U.S. education policy leaders called for tutoring for all students as a supplement for academic learning. Virtual tutoring, in particular, may provide an important path for connecting students in struggling schools with the outside world. Computer-adaptive tutors can provide guidance for highly structured domains such as algebra and geometry. Khan Academy, of course, provides a leading model for how a community tutoring model might address the needs of a wide range of learners. Programs like Khan Academy can't provide all the advantages of 1:1 tutoring, but they can give students access to a diverse community who can respond to questions and offer structured learning examples. All the arguments in the current debate over outsourcing knowledge work certainly apply here; communication technologies make it possible to deepen the linkage between the continents and shrink the world to meet even the most personal needs for teaching and learning.

In Chapter 9 we address how parents might foster productive uses of technology by their children. Then we return to the issue of how to use technologies to address problems of equity in Chapter 10. Clearly, technology has exacerbated the problem of equity in education, and we need to think carefully about how we can mitigate the problem.

What Does It All Mean?

The consequences of the current educational revolution are just beginning to be felt. Technology-driven venues for learning are springing up everywhere, and technological innovations are having unanticipated influence outside of the public school system. Our brief tour in Chapter 4 through the evolution of public schooling in America showed how we came to identify "learning" with formal schooling. Just as new media technologies are unraveling this common-sense definition, they are also helping weave together a more sophisticated model for organizing teaching and learning.

John Hagel and John Seely Brown (2005) argue that successful businesses need to learn from innovations at the edges of their markets. In times of rapid market changes, they comment that "If we adjust our lenses accordingly, then we will begin to see something remarkable: the edges will reshape and eventually transform the core" (p. 11). For the edges to reform the core of schooling, we will have to become both intelligent consumers and producers of the next-generation learning technologies.

Even those of us who don't embrace technology in our lives currently must understand the possibilities of the new technologies from the inside if we want to guide the future of education. As Don Tapscott (1988, pp. 1–2) argues, "For the first time in history, children are more comfortable, knowledgeable, and literate than their parents about an innovation central to society . . . They are a force for social transformation." In this chapter, we offer suggestions for parents and teachers on how to bridge the considerable generation gap and integrate new learning technologies into existing practices.

WHAT ARE KIDS LEARNING FROM TECHNOLOGY?

The emergence of technology-based learning environments requires parents and teachers to pay attention to how (and what) children learn outside of school and the home. Beyond raising awareness of the new technologies, parents and teachers can begin to appreciate the range of new skills that children develop when immersed in these technologies.

The technology literacy gap begins at home. Kids today spend over 9 hours per day interacting with new media (Common Sense Media, 2015). This is more time than they spend in school, with friends, or sleeping. Every day, entrepreneurs are developing new methods for engaging young people with information and entertainment technologies. Although many parents attempt to limit children's access to media, many confess that they do not really understand how children use the new technologies.

Video games provide the clearest case of the technology generation gap. Many parents (and school leaders) frame the "problem" of video games in terms of addiction and the "corruption of our youth." They rightly worry that many of the games that children are engaged in are violent, and that kids are wasting a lot of time with meaningless games and idle talk while not getting enough physical exercise. Meanwhile, children playing video games develop sophisticated problem-solving and communication skills in virtual worlds beyond the experience of many parents. One way to bridge the gap is to extend the idea of reading with your children to playing with your children. Pick up a controller and take *Hearthstone* or *Minecraft* for a spin; let your children teach you how to play, and raise critical questions about strategies and the purpose of game play.

Another direction that parents can pursue is to encourage their children to join online communities that share their own interests. Different kids may have a passion for dinosaurs, poetry, sports, drawing, astronomy, horses, military history, technology, or other areas. Whatever their interests may be, extended pursuit of them can develop expertise that may be highly valuable in later life. It also may develop their research skills, which can be valuable in many endeavors throughout their lives. Encourage your children to move from consumers to producers in their areas of interest. Nudge them toward creating videos, mods, models, and art about their interests. The Internet allows anyone to find a shared community of interest. Understand the communities that your child wants to follow, and find ways to learn with your child about how to make and share contributions with other community members.

For example, children might pursue a passion for coding through an interest in something like *Episode,* a phone app organized around thousands of interactive narrative stories about teen issues of heartbreak, love, and celebrity. From a parent's perspective, the stories might seem repetitive and heavily focused on the central themes of girls' teen fiction. On closer inspection, though, *Episode* allows users to create their own interactive narratives. The stories are created in a relatively sophisticated building process. Users must create three stories of 400 lines of code each(!!) in order to post anything to the *Episode* portal. In order to create a story, users must be able to manipulate graphics, edit sounds, create and code objects within the system, use recursion, and master Hypertext Markup Language (HTML) syntax. In other words, *Episode* builds on the interests of teens and preteens to engage them in a fully developed coding environment. *Episode* claims 8.3 million registered creators, with over 73,000 user-created stories. Even if the initial passion for learning appears dubious to adults, the resulting media skills can create a powerful bridge toward 21st-century literacies.

The virtue of communities of kids with shared passions is that they can take place without any involvement of schools, and with little adult involvement. If adult mentors do participate in the groups, they should probably stay in the background, while encouraging the children to go in new directions that they might not explore on their own. Because the online communities tap into children's passions, they should be self-sustaining, and the community will encourage children to learn deeply about a subject that they care about. If you question how your child learning about coding in *Episode* will help them get a "real job," consider how much attention organizations ranging from the National Science Foundation to New York City public schools pay to creating pathways for science and technology careers for young women. Society values pathways toward 21st-century skills that arise from deep expertise in a subject area.

A common concern expressed by parents and teachers is that time online comes at the expense of reading books. Literacy researchers have long recognized the importance of the early development of rich, functional vocabularies to fuel language development. While solitary reading has always been a steady, gradual path to a larger vocabulary, talking about what you read with people who have larger vocabularies greatly accelerates development. James Paul Gee, an educational linguist, suggests that video games can provide engines for vocabulary development (Gee, 2003). Just as with reading, however, the games themselves provide slow vocabulary acquisition. But when players participate in a larger gaming community, games can offer more opportunities for children to develop new sources of vocabulary in meaningful contexts.

It is difficult to predict how the new technologies will affect more advanced literacy skills, such as finding information and interpreting visual representations. Policymakers interested in preparing students for success in the 21st-century economy, however, would do well to appreciate how skills developed through navigating virtual environments might pay off in the workplace. In *Got Game: How the Gamer Generation Is Shaping Business Forever*, John C. Beck and Mitchell Wade (2004) suggest that the new skills and dispositions of the gamer generation will transform the workplace. The gamer generation will push for work environments to incorporate more virtual aspects into fields such as market analysis and social and economic modeling. Gamers, for example, have abundant experience making big decisions, coordinating resources, and experimenting with complex strategies in game-based simulations. Beck and Wade (2004) also note how gamers have become accustomed to being rewarded for success across multiple game-based environments. This may create pay-for-performance expectations and may make gamers less loyal to companies and more willing to shift to jobs where there are greater challenges. While Beck and Wade's work is attempting to map uncharted territory, it is already clear that the work world of tomorrow will be shaped in part by the gaming technologies of today.

HOW HAS TECHNOLOGY CHANGED KIDS' SOCIAL LIVES AND LEARNING?

The convergence of peer and popular culture through technologies presents possibly the largest threat (and opportunity) for schools and parents. As discussed in Chapter 6, the rise of high schools in the mid-20th century provided the conditions for the emergence of a vibrant peer culture among teens. Beginning in the 1950s, advertisers began to cultivate the lucrative market of teens with disposable income to create pop culture focused on customizing music, style, sports, and movies for teen audiences. Youth participation in pop culture provided a compelling alternative to the social experience of schooling as organized by adults—by the 1960s, millions of teens went to school primarily to associate with friends rather than to get an education. Entertainment technologies fueled the development of pop culture—record players, radios, televisions, and 8-track car stereos are the clear precedents for iPhones, PCs, and tablets. The adolescent (and now preadolescent) embrace of these new technologies has reinforced peer cultures through the development of new jargon—from hip-hop slang to texting conventions—that make the technologies more desirable by promising exclusivity to those in the know.

American pop culture has became a powerful economic engine, generating thousands of jobs and millions of dollars around the world. In fact, pop culture, in the form of music, sports, style, movies, and video games, now provides some of America's leading exports. The explosion of American pop culture displays the fundamental signature of an information economy to generate goods and services, not through the previously dominant method of harnessing raw materials, but instead through the packaging and marketing of human resources as valuable commodities in their own right. In this sense, the pop culture industry presaged the computing boom of the 1980s and 1990s by generating an immense industry from attractive ideas rather than from resources dug from the earth.

The titans of the entertainment industry are currently locked in battle with Internet upstarts on issues around digital distribution and ownership. But the battle over who controls the media may take a back seat to the role of participation in new forms of entertainment. If pop culture can generate substantial economic growth around the world, how will familiarity with pop culture pay off? In other words, will all those evenings watching television or playing Xbox turn into good jobs?

Steven Johnson (2005) suggests that the recent content of media is advancing a new, cognitively demanding form of participatory media literacy right before our eyes. Television shows such as *Game of Thrones* and *Breaking Bad* involve multiple narrative threads that unfold across episodes, while reality shows break open traditional narrative paths by allowing participants to determine the arc. Viewers create websites just to follow along with the show, as well as to discuss plot twists and write stories about their favorite characters. The video game rests at the top of the cognitive complexity chart, as players must solve complex problems using a variety of strategies over the course of dozens or even hundreds of hours to complete the game. As the information economy continues its turn toward the production of virtual environments, experience with the nuances of the new media might lead to informed production, as well as informed consumption. Blogging and crowdsourced news sites are taken seriously by established news networks, and we will see whether the entertainment industry will be revolutionized by participatory media or will succeed in reducing the new media to current forms of production and control.

WHERE DOES THIS LEAVE US?

We advise technological skeptics that they might be looking in the wrong place for change in the core practices of education. Researchers such as Larry Cuban (2001, 2013) have looked for, and have not found, the influence of technological innovation in the classroom. Instead, technological innovation is breaking out in the administrative office with data systems and among students with gaming, leaving teachers behind to maintain their traditional classroom practices.

The pressure to change the classroom with computing is coming from inside and outside schools. To be sure, the trivial implementation of new technologies as supplements to the existing system will continue—there will still be plenty of math homework websites. But the power of new media technologies to transform learning will continue to challenge our schools to do business in new ways. Schools will change internally and become part of larger public-private networks of educational services. Schools will change into new kinds of technologically rich systems.

The new system, unfortunately, may not mark a victory for technology enthusiasts. Even with the implementation of Khan Academy, MOOCs, and Wikipedia, educators and policymakers may continue to focus on teaching basic skills as the core mission of schooling. Enthusiasts who anticipate the natural emergence of change in schools would do well to study the existing structures of schooling to identify the aspects of the current system that are ripe for innovation.

This is the time for technological visionaries to act. We are now at the same stage in the second educational revolution that we were in during the last decades of the 19th century. The central pieces of the emerging system—kindergarten, high schools, graded curricula, and textbooks—were already in existence and beginning to coalesce into a new system. It took a strong local push in districts like St. Louis, New York, and Boston, together with an emerging new field of study in educational administration and psychology, to fit these pieces together to make the "one-best system." Now we face a similar swirl of new pieces of a potential system—computer-adaptive learning tools, video games, distributed networks, and maker spaces. We need strong leadership from innovative educators to make sure that this new system embodies our society's critical goals for education.

CHAPTER 10

Rethinking Education in a Technological World

A vision for a new education system is just over the horizon. To realize it, political and educational leaders will need to mobilize resources to take advantage of the great power of the learning tools that have emerged to transform education for all learners.

Since the end of World War II, the United States has enjoyed a disproportionate share of global resources. This abundance allowed Americans to maintain a high standard of living and take a world leadership role. Thomas Friedman's (2006) *The World Is Flat: A Brief History of the Twenty-First Century* suggests that access to information technologies has leveled the global playing field. This leveling is allowing millions of engineers, technologists, and professionals from around the world to pursue the careers that have made so many Americans wealthy. The future prosperity of countries around the world depends on how education systems can take advantage of new technologies to foster learning for all citizens. If the United States is going to lead the global economy, it will have to reinvent education to embrace the potential of new media tools as core practices.

The formula for economic success has a high cost. As has happened in the United States, countries that focus on knowledge economies as the source of wealth generation tend to concentrate economic resources in an elite class. The gap between the haves and have-nots is growing around the world, and elite populations are more motivated than ever to preserve their privilege by dominating preparation for math, science, and technology careers. Global competition for what is perceived as a diminished opportunity to be on the top has sparked what W. E. B. DuBois called a "top ten percent" education strategy, which concentrates resources for the most talented students to claim globally competitive professions. Gary Orfield and Chungmei Lee (2007) suggest that the resegregation of schools and communities, voucher policies, and charter schools is already pushing our education policy away from its commitment to equity.

Just how technological developments will help us balance the goals of equity and global competition is not yet clear. The rethinking of education that we promote with this book should aim toward strategies that provide access to the new educational resources for everyone in society and give people the motivation to take advantage of these resources. This demands not rethinking education in isolation, but rather considering the interplay of society, education, and learning.

RETHINKING LEARNING

Older adults all grew up with the idea that learning meant going to school. As we argued throughout this book, the identification of education with schooling is slowly unraveling, as new technologies move learning outside of school's walls. In some sense, the divorce of schooling from learning may take us back to an era where individuals negotiate their own learning experiences, often with strong guidance from adults and other professionals in their lives.

Eventually, when people and politicians become worried about what kids are learning or what adults don't know, their automatic reaction may not be "How can we improve the schools?" Instead, they may ask, "How can we help learners to create their own learning pathways?" "How can we make new technology resources available to more people?" or "What kinds of tools can support people to seek out information on their own?" Currently, the strong association between schooling and learning forces our conversation into institutional responses. We don't yet know how to ask these wider questions when we think about improving education. We hope that this book starts that conversation.

As learning moves out of school, our conception of learning will begin to broaden, and we will see more hybrid experiences that begin in the classroom and move back and forth into other learning communities. Education may follow the path of homeschooling by having each student design an idiosyncratic agenda of taking field trips, writing Wikipedia entries, designing computer games, or even teaching others by making and circulating YouTube videos. For example, a programming teacher might be approached by a few of her students who want to bring their own computers into school and hook them up in a network to engage in multiplayer video games with each other. They might form a computer club, where they begin to develop computer games of their own. And as new kids join the club, the first group would teach them things that they had learned. Some of these students might be asked in their English classes to create videos that explain a complex process, so they begin posting videos to explain the most difficult aspects of their video games on a custom YouTube channel. The students then might help design and implement a similar network in the middle school library and begin to tutor younger students on game play and network maintenance. While all this learning might take place in a school setting, it is not "real" school learning. Technology directors around the country are experimenting with similar models that rely on students to learn about hardware, software, gaming, and production.

Our vision of education in this book is structured around the idea of lifelong learning. *Lifelong learning* requires moving away from highly structured schooling institutions and instead acting as participants in a wide variety of learning experiences. Learners will need to develop the skills to judge the quality of learning venues and the kinds of social networks that provide guidance and advice.

Brigid Barron (2006) provides examples of how students learn to become intelligent consumers of learning environments through developing their computer skills. For example, one middle-school girl in California named Stephanie, the daughter of Chinese immigrants, had a group of friends who used GeoCities to create their own webpages. They taught Stephanie how to use Hypertext Markup Language (HTML), which appealed to her because she liked to draw. Then, in seventh grade, she took courses in programming, web design, and industrial technology, where she used a computer to create designs. In eighth grade, she decided to develop a webpage for her family and helped her father design a webpage for his new business. She even taught her mother different ways to use computers. As she got further into art with the computer, she lurked in the background of Xanga, an online digital-art community, trying to pick up techniques for making computer art. She would study the finished works and the source code that the artists used to produce them. She is a typical self-directed learner in the digital age.

Social networks show how technologies can replicate the support and guidance functions of schools. These networks draw people across all ages from very different backgrounds—some quite expert and others very inexperienced. Some learn by hanging out in the background, and others by asking questions. Groups in the network may jointly investigate topics of interest or argue about issues that they think are important. The successful sites, however, share the characteristic of providing information to guide the interests of users. Online affinity groups exist for every known disease and disorder, and doctors across the country know that their diagnoses are checked by an increasingly informed patient population. These kinds of social networks are blossoming around topics of particular interest to different groups of people, such as poetry, chemistry, digital graphics, and fantasy sports.

What might happen if our thinking about schooling doesn't change? If schools can't change fast enough to keep pace with advances in learning technologies, learning will leave schooling behind. We see this happening outside the United States already. For example, with inexpensive computers, young people in Thailand and Brazil can have access to the same resources for learning that people in the developed world now have. Many will choose to take advantage of these resources to escape poverty. In some ways, they will be a new kind of 21st-century immigrant—instead of moving to a new country, they will use information networks to transform their thinking. They will be able to find like-minded souls to share ideas in cyberspace. English will likely be their common language, which they will pick up from the web.

As older generations continue to inflict established methods of learning on younger generations in the name of high-quality education, new technologies will continue to lure learners into exciting, interest-based environments. Schools will continue to serve learners and families who see the advantage of the credentials offered by the traditional pathways to learning. But the most innovative energy for learning will emerge in the technology environments that spring up outside of schools.

RETHINKING MOTIVATION

The current school system does not help students develop intrinsic motivation to learn. The disengagement experienced by many students is reinforced by less-than-ideal classroom experiences. One report found that 50% of high school students are bored every day in their classes (Yazzie-Mintz, 2006); another found that 82% of 9th and 10th graders in California reported their school experiences as "boring and irrelevant" (Hart, 2006). Changing these deeply ingrained attitudes about learning will mean changing both the process of teaching and learning and the reward system for successful completion of schooling.

Fortunately, learning technologies provide some direction about how to improve student motivation to learn and to invigorate learning content. To produce a generation of people who seek out learning, learners need more control over their own learning. Learner control can be fostered by giving kids the tools to support their learning, such as access to the web, machines for toddlers that teach reading, tutoring help when needed, and computer-based games that foster deep knowledge and entrepreneurial skills.

A love of learning also can be fostered by encouraging kids to explore deeply topics in which they are particularly interested, as homeschooling parents do. Kurt Squire (2004, 2006) found that kids who play real-time strategy games, such as *Civilization,* begin to check out books on ancient cultures and earn better grades in middle school. Instead of diverting student attention from schools, as feared by many teachers and school leaders, video games can provide a path to make conventional school content more appealing and encourage students to give their classroom instruction another chance. By understanding how new technologies can encourage kids to take responsibility for their own learning, society may help to produce a generation of people who seek out ways to learn.

Pushing students to take more control of their learning, as we have discussed, runs counter to the institutional control of learning exercised by schools. Fostering self-directed learning will require challenging the current policy assumptions that pressure schools to teach everyone the same thing at the same time. Even the one-room schools that preceded universal schooling resisted this contemporary impulse to standardize instruction. Integrating computers into the center of schooling, rather than at the periphery, could help learners pursue individualized, interactive lessons with adequate support. Such systems can control the level of challenge by choosing tasks that reflect the learner's recent history. Teachers can help when students need more assistance than the computer can provide. Such individualized learning would remove the stigma of looking bad when you don't understand something that others grasp.

Technologies also point to another path toward fostering a love of learning through design and production. Savvy computer game developers have long realized that access to tools for redesigning the game environment greatly increases the replay value and brand loyalty of their games. By giving students meaningful tasks to accomplish, they will understand why they are doing what they are doing. Students who struggle in school spend hundreds of hours creating interactive narratives on *Episode* or editing gaming videos on YouTube. Suddenly, when the drudge work of complicated tasks becomes contextualized and has new significance, students are more than willing to take the time to "get it right." As a society, we need to understand how new technologies turn kids and adults on to learning in order to redesign our learning environments to provide positive motivational experiences for all learners.

RETHINKING WHAT IS IMPORTANT TO LEARN

Of course, providing intrinsic motivation to learn also requires us to rethink the rewards of successfully completing a course of learning. There is a mismatch between the programs that schools offer and the kinds of skills that are needed to live a successful life in a knowledge economy (Collins, 2017). The core curriculum in modern schools is still rooted in the medieval *trivium* (from which the word *trivial* is derived), which consisted of logic, grammar, and rhetoric, and *quadrivium*, which was made up of arithmetic, geometry, music, and astronomy. These formed the bases for the liberal arts, which dominate the current course of study in school and college. Over the centuries, we added courses such as history, geography, and the sciences, but the basic organization of the curriculum reflects its historical roots.

A question that society must wrestle with is whether this is the best curriculum for preparing students to live in an age with rich technological resources. Proponents of traditional curricula argue that classical training in thinking and writing is needed now more than ever; progressive educators suggest that new literacy skills and mathematical reasoning skills are needed for new times. In schools, however, the compromise between the two camps is often to organize content roughly into classical disciplines, but to remove the rigor and the context from the classical content. Thus, geometry is presented without a sense of history, and sciences are learned as sets of facts instead of methods to organize observations and experiments. Because we think of education as what goes on in school, this compromise curriculum furnishes a narrow and quite impoverished view of what is important to learn.

There are two areas in which the new technological resources clearly affect what is important to learn: communication and mathematics. In 21st-century communication practices, boundaries are becoming blurred between core literacy practices, such as learning to read and write, and more applied production and presentation practices. Creating multimedia documents, presenting yourself on social media sites, putting together and critiquing videos, finding information and resources on the web, and understanding images and graphics are all becoming important aspects of communication.

New technologies offer interesting ways to make the transition between basic and applied literacies. For example, people who play massively multiplayer online games (MMOGs), such as *World of Warcraft*, develop a whole range of applied skills, such as negotiation, forming alliances, strategizing and outwitting opponents, calculating which approach is most likely to work, and communicating with different kinds of people. These applied literacy skills occur naturally in MMOGs, but are difficult to foster in traditional school environments. Yet because we think of literacy skill development as directly tied to traditional school content, most people regard gamers as wasting their time playing these MMOGs.

In terms of mathematics, technology can carry out all the algorithms that students spend so much time learning in school. At the same time, learning to think mathematically is more important than ever. Therefore, students' time might be better spent in learning how to use mathematical tools to solve real-world problems rather than learning how to mimic computer algorithms. In fact, understanding how to apply computer tools appropriately requires much more thinking than executing algorithms. It should become the new agenda for teaching mathematics.

Fantasy sports present a pathway for teaching applied mathematical skills. Calculating on-base percentages or adding up runs scored may not involve sophisticated algorithmic processes, but even the most casual fantasy baseball player must engage in predictive models to anticipate which players and teams have the best chance to succeed. Having fantasy players articulate their predictive models is an excellent exercise in developing the kinds of estimation and number sense skills prized by organizations such as the National Council of Teachers of Mathematics.

A subtle impact of technology on learning has to do with the easy availability of knowledge. In the past, people have had to memorize information to make competent decisions, as doctors must do to make accurate diagnoses. But with easy access to knowledge, they can rely more on external data to help them. We can illustrate this phenomenon with the use of technology by doctors. Online systems have been developed to help doctors make diagnoses. Doctors can feed the systems with sets of symptoms, and the systems can suggest possible diagnoses the doctors should consider. That way, the doctor does not have to remember every possible pairing of symptoms to diagnoses. But they still must apply their personal knowledge, gained from experience and from interaction with the patient, to make their decisions. These systems act as memory aids.

Similarly, the web is a huge memory aid, in addition to providing new information on every topic under the sun. The essential skill is no longer memorization, but knowing how to find the information that you want on the web, including how to evaluate what you find, given the differences in reliability among websites. That is to say, people need to develop new learning skills rather than just acquire more information.

RETHINKING CAREERS

While education has traditionally aimed to enlighten learners about their political responsibilities, American discussions of education have turned sharply toward career preparation for economic success. But as routine jobs are replaced by technology or shipped offshore, the remaining jobs emphasize collaboration, communication, and knowledge-processing skills. From an economic perspective, it's imperative for education to focus much more on teaching students how to think critically in a digital age, as well as how to find the knowledge and resources that they need to accomplish difficult tasks. Students would be better served if they were challenged to solve real-world problems like the obesity epidemic and create meaningful strategies to address them. Then they might have some incentive to learn how to think.

Career mobility also challenges educational institutions to teach students to become more adaptive. The traditional American story was that we went to school to prepare ourselves for a career, whether as an auto mechanic or a doctor. We would settle on a career sometime during high school or college and take courses geared toward success in that career. In the 1980s and 1990s, however, the erosion of corporate responsibility for lifetime employment sparked increased job mobility across the economy. Fifty to 60% of new hires leave their jobs within the first year, and 10% of the workforce leave their jobs every year (Feller & Walz, 1996; Henkoff, 1996). As we live longer, it turns out that many of us may be working into our 70s and 80s. Most Americans in the next 20 years will likely have a succession of careers.

As an example, the first author started his career as an auditor on Wall Street after getting a college degree in accounting. After a few years as an auditor, he returned to graduate school in computer and communication sciences, and 10 years later, he graduated with a PhD in cognitive psychology. After that, he went to work in a research firm that carried out research for the federal government in a variety of areas, most related to the use of computers in society. In his work, he slowly moved from doing psychological research to developing computer systems for education. After some 20 years in research, he joined the education faculty at Northwestern, never having taken an education course during his career. Then, for 18 more years, he taught a variety of education courses at Northwestern. For his part, the second author started as a graduate student in philosophy. He took a job as a history teacher in a small Chicago school. After several years of teaching, he became an administrator at the school. Later, he decided to return to graduate school in education. After spending five more years in graduate school, he became a professor at a large graduate school of education.

These stories, while they focus on academic careers, are not unusual. Such twists and turns in careers are becoming more and more common. The fate of people in a knowledge society, it seems, is that they must keep reinventing themselves to keep up with the changing world around them.

Eventually, people will come to think of life as made up of a succession of careers. To cope with this idea, they will begin to see how important it is to "learn how to learn." They may come to see that the career that they decide to pursue in their early years is not a commitment for life. As Avner Ahitov and Robert Lerman (2004) point out, "Every month, millions of workers leave one employer and take a job with another employer. It takes young workers a long time to enter a stable career and a long-term relationship with an employer. By the age of 30, high school graduates with no college have already worked for an average of eight employers. Nearly half of all male high school graduates experienced at least one spell of unemployment between ages 25–29. Moreover, job instability is increasing among young men" (p. 1).

There has been a growing gap between the incomes of college graduates and high school graduates. This has led over 90% of high school students to plan to go to college. But only 14% of kids with a C average in high school will complete a college degree (Rosenbaum, 1989, 2001). They would be better off working for a few years after they finish high school and then going back to get more education if they wish. The success in college of returning veterans after World War II testifies to the payoff in waiting to go to college. A study by Norman Frederiksen (1950) found that the veterans had higher achievement levels than nonveterans. Some of the pressure to go right on to college will be relieved if people come to understand that their life in the future will likely alternate between working and learning. It will no longer be 15 or 20 years of preparation, followed by 30 years of working. Rather, we will learn for a while, work for a while, change jobs, learn about new possibilities, work again, and repeat indefinitely.

Of course, some people in the future may be actors or auto mechanics for all their lives. But they will be the exceptions. Thinking of a single career as the standard pattern leads people to think that they are done with learning when they finish school. So they do not keep their minds open and focused on continuing their learning. This makes them less adaptable when hit with the necessity of changing careers. Parents also need to understand how the nature of people's careers have changed and not try to force young people to prepare for a particular career that they think is best for them. As a society, we need policies that support people in making the many career transitions that they will have to make in a constantly changing environment.

RETHINKING THE TRANSITIONS BETWEEN LEARNING AND WORK

America does not have a well-developed apprenticeship system. Both high school graduates who don't enter college and students who drop out of college early enter the workforce unprepared. Since only about

30% of students in America ever get a college degree, the vast majority of students have a more difficult transition to make. Typically, they drift from job to job until they are 25 or 30. Some return to college when they are older, but it is often harder for these students because the society does not support older people returning to college. Given the increasing centrality of technology in work and the fact that people are more and more likely to change careers several times during their lifetime, it is worth rethinking the ways that society supports the transitions between learning and work.

The transition to work is handled fairly well when people graduate from college. The colleges maintain an office designed to help students find jobs, both as interns during college and when they graduate. This office has extensive files on employers in their area, and many have files of alumni employed in different occupations who can guide students in choosing a career. Employers come to the colleges to recruit graduating students who are interested in working for them. Often, college students intern for different employers during the summer or during one of their later semesters, thus forging ties with potential employers after they graduate. And college professors often write letters of recommendation for their students, even pointing them to potential employers that they know. High school career centers and teachers sometimes perform this function, but it is sporadic and concentrated in wealthier communities. So there is an effective system in place, but only for college graduates.

In an era of multiple careers, people will need support to navigate their options in going both from learning to work and from work to learning. If America wants to remain a successful society, it needs to create new ways to support citizens through these challenging transitions.

We believe that America must transform how we address technical and vocational education. For example, schools should reconsider how to support teenagers who want to go into the job market, either in addition to or instead of going to high school. Teens should have access to personalized learning counselors who can advise about available educational options. As learning becomes more critical for success in the world, people will need individual support from someone who knows their history and the particulars of their lives. Technologies greatly expand the range of advice that counselors can use to guide learners. Counselors can direct learners to online resources that guide novices through the initial stages of career choice and development.

Teenagers should not go to work until they have mastered the basic skills and knowledge taught in middle school. High school guidance programs should move toward measuring whether teenagers have met the standards for going to work and help them find jobs that are well suited to their goals and abilities. This office would keep files of possible jobs, just as college employment offices do, help students put together résumés and assess their interests and abilities, and help gather teacher recommendations and make initial contacts with employers. In short, this office would carry out many of the same functions as college employment offices, but provide more guidance because the students are younger. Modest federal funding in this area would provide significant value in helping students make a successful transition between learning and work.

The same office might administer apprenticeship programs, such as are widely found in Europe (Hamilton, 1990; Olson, 1997). In these programs, adolescent students typically work three days a week and go to school for two days a week. The programs attempt to coordinate what students are learning in school with the work for which they are training. A more robust apprenticeship system also might support students who have gone to work and wish to return to full- or part-time learning. The office could advise them of their options, such as taking high school or community college classes, online courses, or courses administered by a local learning center.

Such offices also can serve adults, who need help in thinking about embarking on a new career or returning to get more education. These counseling offices might be maintained by the state in all the high schools, or they might be privately run. They would have counselors who can advise people on the kind of training and credentials that they need to pursue a particular career, and what kind of educational resources are available to pursue that training. Other counselors could assess the skills and interests of adults to guide them toward viable careers that they might pursue. Still other counselors would have knowledge and contacts with employers in the region and could help people find a job that suits them, given their training and interests. These are resources that we need to provide to people to make our society as productive as possible.

Apprenticeship systems should receive the same levels of support as traditional public schools. School-to-work programs, such as the School-to-Work Opportunities Act, provide a good start toward institutionalizing these types of services. Building better transitional services means that students with the least social capital, who need the most help connecting to viable economic resources, will receive assistance in making job connections. There are so many alternatives that it is bewildering for most people, so they need counseling to make wise decisions. We will all profit from others learning all they can and finding employment that suits them.

RETHINKING EDUCATIONAL LEADERSHIP

We are experiencing a time of educational transition, which demands a new kind of educational leadership—a new Horace Mann, as it were. We need a vision of education that makes it possible for the new array of educational resources to reach all the people. The trends in place are reaching the elites, leaving behind the vast majority of people. The next generation of education leaders will need to face the political and technological challenges. The challenges of changing a well-established, entrenched institution are far different than those faced by Horace Mann. Parents, teachers, policymakers, and local communities all have compelling reasons to preserve the current system. Forces for change, such as the civil rights emphasis on using schools to increase social equity and the technological emphasis to open the core practices of schooling to information technologies, push uncomfortably against influential conservative stakeholders. Leaders who can effect real change need to understand where the leverage points are in order to move the system, and need to have the organizational skills to bring together the necessary resources and skills to create change.

One possibility is to promote policies that put computing and online access in the hands of all students and families. Such policies provide access to a vast array of educational resources for nonelites. But limiting schools with the most need to the least adventurous learning programs will undercut the power of access to new media tools. Simply inserting technology into high-poverty classrooms and schools, without considering how the contexts for learning need to change, will likely fail. Leaders need to understand the power of the new technologies, as well as the limits of instructional programs designed only to raise test scores, to establish ambitious expectations for their communities. They will need to think about how to bring coherence to the incoherent array of tools already in schools and in the world.

In the future, educational leadership will require more than just re-forming schools. We need to think about how to integrate non-school resources into learning environments, supporting families both in bringing these tools into their homes and in building wired learning centers in communities that reach those in need. Tablet computers present an accessible opportunity to provide age-appropriate virtual learning resources for all learners. A new generation of apps supports robust, language-rich resources, which very young kids can use to learn to read. Apps allow learners to hear a Dr. Seuss story by point-ing at the words or lines on the screen to have them read aloud. As the kids learn the sight-to-sound correspondences, they will pick up reading their favorite stories on their own. Tablets can direct learners toward the best children's literature covering a wide variety of genres and topics, as well as games to teach basic mathematical operations to young kids. Every young child should have such a machine, which provides a variety of educational resources.

Elementary schools should take advantage of computer-adaptive learning tools to provide supplementary learning services to help students having trouble. These programs can be powerful comple-ments to the Response to Intervention models widely used to address student learning needs. If a child is having trouble in writing or math, computer-adaptive learning tools can provide a customized diagnosis that connects her or his learning needs with appropriate resources. These same technologies allow students to use programs at home with their families, as well as at school.

After eighth grade, kids might follow different educational paths depending on their own and their parents' choosing. For example, as an alternative to continuing to a traditional high school, a student might take online courses at home or in a learning center, enter an apprenticeship program, take courses at a community college, or attend a Career Academy that organizes the curriculum around particular career interests, such as medicine or technology. Many cities, such as Oakland, California, have developed Career Academies in a number of different areas. The kids might even work for a while and later return to get more education when they are ready. By giving students such options, they are less likely to feel that high school is a prison that they must endure until they are grown up enough to go out on their own.

As mentioned previously, all schools should have a staff of learning counselors who can develop a personalized pathway for each student. The visits to a counselor while in school should be free and routine for everyone 14 years old and above. Learning counselors would be trained and licensed by the state, just as medical doctors are. The goal would be to develop a learning plan to address each person's interests, needs, and abilities. The plan would be adapted over the years as the person changed jobs and acquired more knowledge and responsibilities. As stated previously, the learning plan might involve taking online courses, going to a learning center for specialized training, getting a technical certification in some area, joining an apprenticeship program, or learning from computer-based tutorials to enhance particular skills. In any case, the learner should check with the counselor at regular intervals to evaluate how things are going and to consider how the plan might be revised.

These examples show how educational leaders need to think about changing schools from within, and how learners can be linked to resources outside schools. Thinking more broadly about technologies can revive our ideas about equity and extend available resources to the nonelites in our society. Our proposals are merely suggestive of the issues that leaders should be considering. Because society has identified education with schooling, we are systematically overlooking many of the resources now available for helping minorities and other nonelites.

Further, society views education reform as something that applies to youth rather than to people of all ages. With a broader view of education, we can begin to think about how to provide educational resources to people in their 50s, 60s, 70s, and beyond.

We are not going to fix education by fixing the schools. They have served us very well in the past, but they are a 19th-century invention trying to cope with a 21st-century society. This is the time for another Horace (or Leticia) Mann to step forward and lead the nation toward a new education system. Our new leaders will have to understand the affordances of the new technologies and to watch for opportunities for implementation. They will need to understand that learning does not start with kindergarten and end with a high school or college diploma—that we need to design a coherent lifelong-learning system.

RETHINKING THE ROLE OF GOVERNMENT IN EDUCATION

Historically, states, cities, and towns have been responsible for education in America, with the federal government playing only a supplementary role. The federal government has carried out some programs, such as developing science and math curricula to make the nation more competitive or supporting poor children by providing resources to ensure greater equity among children. But teacher salaries, curriculum materials, and administrative expenses were paid with local funds. Many perceive federally imposed education standards on states, cities, and towns as an encroachment on local authority. As the pendulum swings back toward local control, states will try to protect their authority, which leads to a backlash against centralized initiatives such as the Common Core State Standards and federal guidelines on school accountability.

As we have pointed out, new technologies introduce inequities into the education system. Wealthier parents are buying tutoring, computers, and web access for their children, leaving poor children further behind than ever. States currently do not commit the resources to correct these imbalances. They get most of their monies for education from property taxes, and fewer and fewer households are willing to raise property taxes sufficiently to pay for the education of all children.

Without stepping on the states' authority, the federal government can try to equalize educational opportunities for all citizens. They can provide incentives to develop and use computer-adaptive teaching and learning tools and subsidize computers for all families. They can provide educational guidance and tutoring for those who can't afford to buy these services. They can fund apprenticeship programs that help kids make the transition into the uncertain vocational world. They can pay for additional training when people want to change careers. These are all supplemental services that support states' authority and encourage new directions for education services.

There is also an important new role for state government in bringing about a new vision of education for a technology-rich world. If our society is going to support new alternatives for pursuing education, the states need to rethink their mandates of keeping kids in comprehensive school until they are 16 years old. If we are going to let teenagers pursue other options besides staying in high school, the states will need to specify what alternatives are acceptable instead of school and what requirements people must meet before pursuing each alternative.

For example, the state might mandate that students acquire a specific set of certificates, such as demonstrating an ability to read and do math at an eighth-grade level, before they can pursue a full-time job or some other option as an alternative to high school. The states also might monitor teenagers' performance on the job and require them to attend a weekly class where they discuss what they have learned in their work. If the work is not serving as a learning experience for these teens, a guidance counselor may help them find a new job that has more value to them. If students are taking online courses at a learning center or participating in an apprenticeship program, the state might monitor their progress in a similar fashion. The state would still have a responsibility for teenagers, but it would give them more latitude in pursuing their own education.

We have outlined examples of possible responsibilities that governments could take on, but these are not definitive. Governments should provide guidance to students at the same time that they loosen the reins that are keeping kids in high school, which many of them view as a kind of prison. It would be wise for governments to put more responsibility on learners to pursue their own learning, but at the same time, it is critical that government not ignore its responsibility to provide equal access to educational resources for all citizens.

OUR VISION OF THE FUTURE

As education becomes more privatized and commercial, we risk losing the vision promulgated by Thomas Jefferson and Horace Mann of a society where everyone has an equal chance at a good education. Horace Mann was right in predicting that education could provide a path for everyone to become part of the elite. Universal schooling formed the basis for our middle-class society today. But the onset of technology, privatization, and increasing inequality of income is undermining this vision.

Making economic success the central outcome of schooling risks marginalizing the political and moral goals of education. Education is, in many ways, America's civic religion. We use education to work toward our national ideals of equality, opportunity, and democracy. As a society, we need to understand how to balance the need to use schools as engines of economic competition with our national commitment to equality of opportunity.

Those of us who care about education should do whatever we can to see that our children are educated as best they can to prepare them to live in a technology-rich society. Even those of us without children should pay attention to this trend. All of us depend on the next generation to support our social services, such as Social Security and Medicare. For the future of America and the welfare of our individual futures, it is important that our society invest in the next generation's education. It behooves all of us to work toward a more equitable system of education.

What role will technology play in our national story of equity and economic development? In the 19th century, Americans developed the public school system to institutionalize our national commitment to citizenship, while at the same time addressing the needs of families to care for and educate children in the midst of the Industrial Revolution. Our generation faces a similar but radically new design challenge. We are dealing with a mature, stable system of education designed to adapt to gradual change, but ill suited to embrace radical change. The pace of technological change has outstripped the ability of school systems to adapt essential practices. Schools have fiddled with learning technologies on the margins of the system, in boutique innovations that leave core practices untouched. The emergence of new forms of teaching and learning outside of school threatens the identification of learning with formal schooling forged in the 19th century.

For education to embrace both equity and economic development, we believe that our leaders will have to stretch their traditional practices to embrace the capacity of new information technologies. This will require schools to forfeit some control over learning processes, but also once again will put the latest tools for improving learning in the hands of public institutions (as opposed to the hands of families and learners who can afford access).

Parents and citizens need to start pushing for this more-expansive view of education reform. School leaders and teachers will need to understand how learning technologies work and how they change the basic interactions of teachers and learners. Technology leaders will need to work together with educators, not as missionaries bearing magical gifts, but as collaborators in creating new opportunities to learn.

It will take a concerted effort to bring about such a radical change in thinking. If a broader view develops in society, leaders will emerge who can bring about the political changes necessary to make new educational resources available to everyone. These new leaders will need to understand the affordances of the new technologies and have a vision for education that will bring the new resources to everyone. We hope these leaders may be reading this book now, and that it can guide them in taking action to address the learning revolution that is upon us.

References

American Youth Policy Forum. (2002). *Florida Virtual School: The future of learning?* Retrieved from aypf.org/forumbriefs/2002/fb101802.htm

Amrein, A. L., & Berliner, D. C. (2002). High-stakes testing, uncertainty, and student learning. *Education Policy Analysis Archives, 10*(18). Retrieved from epaa.asu.edu /epaa/v10n18/

Anderson, J. R., Boyle, C. F., & Reiser, B. J. (1985). Intelligent tutoring systems. *Science, 228*, 456–468.

Anderson, M. (2017). *Digital divide persists even as lower-income Americans make gains in tech adoption.* Pew Research Center. Retrieved from pewresearch. org/fact-tank/2017/03/22/digital-divide-persists-even-as-lower-income-americans-make-gains-in-tech-adoption/

Avituv, A., & Lerman, R. I. (2004). *Job turnover, wage rates, and marriage stability: How are they related?* New York: Urban Institute. Retrieved from urban. org/publications/411148.html

Barron, B. (2006). Interest and self-sustained learning as catalysts of development: A learning ecologies perspective. *Human Development, 49*(4), 193–224.

Barron, B., Gomez, K., Pinkard, N., & Martin, C. K. (2014). *The digital youth network: Cultivating digital citizenship in urban communities.* Cambridge, MA: MIT Press.

Beck, J. C., & Wade, M. (2004). *Got game: How the gamer generation is shaping business forever.* Cambridge, MA: Harvard Business School Press.

Black, R. W. (2008). *Adolescents and online fan fiction.* New York: Peter Lang.

Bonney, R., Phillips, T. B., Enck, J., Shirk. J., & Trautmann, N. (2014). *Citizen science and youth education.* Commissioned by the Committee on Successful Out-of-School Learning, National Academies of Arts & Sciences. Retrieved from sites.nationalacademies.org/cs/groups/dbassesite/documents/webpage/dbasse_089993.pdf

Boyd, D. (2014). *It's complicated: The social lives of networked teens.* New Haven, CT: Yale University Press.

Brooks, D. (2004). *On Paradise Drive: How we live now (and always have) in the future tense.* New York: Simon & Schuster.

Brown, J. S. (1985, Spring). Idea amplifiers: New kinds of electronic learning environments. *Educational Horizons,* 108–112.

Brown, J. S. (2007). Innovation and technology: Interview. *Wired.* Retrieved from johnseelybrown.com/wired_int.html

Brown, J. S., & Thomas, D. (2006, April). You play *Warcraft?* You're hired! *Wired, 14*(4). Retrieved from wired.com/2006/04/learn/

Burch, P. (2010). The bigger picture: Institutional perspectives on interim assessment technologies. *Peabody Journal of Education, 85,* 147–162.

Callahan, R. E. (1962). *Education and the cult of efficiency.* Chicago, IL: University of Chicago Press.

Carlton, F. T. (1965). *Economic influences upon educational progress in the United States, 1820–1850.* Richmond, VA: William Byrd Press. (Originally published 1908.)

Carnoy, M., & Levin, H. (1985). *Schooling and work in the democratic state.* Stanford, CA: Stanford University Press.

Carr, N. (2011). *The shallows: What the Internet is doing to our brains.* New York: W. W. Norton.

Chau, C. (2010). YouTube as a participatory culture. *New Directions in Youth Development, 128,* 65–74. doi: 10.1002/yd.376

Cohen, D. K. (1988a). Educational technology and school organization. In R. S. Nickerson & P. Zodhiates (Eds.), *Technology and education: Looking toward 2020* (pp. 231–264). Mahwah, NJ: Lawrence Erlbaum Associates.

Cohen, D. K. (1988b). Teaching practice: Plus ça change. . . . In P. Jackson (Ed.), *Contributing to educational change: Perspectives on research and practice* (pp. 27–84). Berkeley, CA: McCutchan.

Coleman, J. S. (1961). *The adolescent society.* New York: Free Press.

Collins, A. (1991). Cognitive apprenticeship and instructional technology. In L. Idol & B. F. Jones (Eds.), *Educational values and cognitive instruction: Implications for reform* (pp. 119–136). Hillsdale, NJ: Lawrence Erlbaum Associates.

Collins, A. (2017). *What's worth teaching: Rethinking curriculum in the age of technology.* New York: Teachers College Press.

Collins, A., & Brown, J. S. (1988). The computer as a tool for learning through reflection. In H. Mandl & Lesgold (Eds.), *Learning issues for intelligent tutoring systems* (pp. 1–18). New York: Springer-Verlag.

Collins, A., Neville, P., & Bielaczyc, K. (2000). The role of different media in designing learning environments. *International Journal of Artificial Intelligence in Education, 11,* 144–162.

Common Sense Media. (2015). *Media use by teens and tweens.* Retrieved from commonsensemedia.org/research/the-common-sense-census-media-use-by-tweens-and-teens

Conlan, M. (2016, May 24). *What you might have missed at Maker Faire Bay Area 2016.* Retrieved from edtechmagazine.com/k12/article/2016/05/ed-tech-innovations-you-missed-maker-faire-bay-area-2016

Corbett, A. T., Koedinger, K. R., & Anderson, J. R. (1997). Intelligent tutoring systems. In M. Helander, T. K. Landauer, & P. Prabhu (Eds.), *Handbook of human-computer interaction* (pp. 849–873). Amsterdam: Elsevier Science.

Cremin, L. A. (1951). *The American common school: An historic conception.* New York: Bureau of Publications, Teachers College, Columbia University.

Cremin, L. A. (1977). *Traditions of American education.* New York: Basic Books.

Cremin, L. A. (1980). *American education: The national experience, 1783–1876.* New York: Harper & Row.

Csikszentmihalyi, M. (1990). *Flow: The psychology of optimal experience.* New York: Harper & Row.

Cuban, L. (1984). *How teachers taught.* New York: Longman.

Cuban, L. (1986). *Teachers and machines.* New York: Teachers College Press.

Cuban, L. (2001). *Oversold and underused: Computers in the classroom.* Cambridge, MA: Harvard University Press.

Cuban, L. (2013). *Inside the black box of classroom practice: Change without reform in American education.* Cambridge, MA: Harvard Education Press.

Cubberley, E. (1916). *Public school administration.* Boston, MA: Houghton Mifflin.

Daiute, C. (1985). *Writing and computers.* Reading, MA: Addison-Wesley.

Davies, S., & Aurini, J. (2006). The franchising of private tutoring: A view from Canada. *Phi Delta Kappan, 88*(2), 123–128.

de Tocqueville, A. (2003). *Democracy in America and two essays on America.* G. E. Bevan, trans. London, UK: Penguin.

Dede, C., Nelson, B., Ketelhut, D., Clarke, J., & Bowman, C. (2004). Design-based research strategies for studying situated learning in a multi-user virtual environment. In *Proceedings of the 2004 International Conference on Learning Sciences* (pp. 158–165). Mahwah, NJ: Lawrence Erlbaum Associates.

Devane, L. (2016, July 29). 14 surprising facts about educators' social media use. *E-School News.* Retrieved from eschoolnews.com/2016/07/29/14-facts-about-educators-social-media-use/

Downes, S. (2012, April 23). Rise of the MOOCs. downes.ca/post/57911

Duncan, G. J., & Murnane, R. J. (2011). The American dream: Then and now. In G. J. Duncan and R. J. Murnane (Eds.), *Whither opportunity? Rising inequality, schools, and children's life chances* (pp. 3–23). San Francisco, CA: Russell Sage.

Dwyer, D. C., Ringstaff, C., & Sandholtz, J. (1990). *The evolution of teachers' instructional beliefs and practices in high-access-to-technology classrooms.* Paper presented at the annual meeting of the American Educational Research Association, Boston, MA.

Eckert, P. (1989). *Jocks and burnouts: Social categories and identity in high school.* New York: Teachers College Press.

Eisenstein, E. L. (1979). *The printing press as an agent of change*. Cambridge, UK: Cambridge University Press.

Enyedy, N. (2014). *Personalized instruction: New interest, old rhetoric, limited results, and the need for a new direction for computer-mediated learning*. Boulder, CO: National Education Policy Center. Retrieved from nepc.colorado.edu/publication/personalized-instruction

Farnham-Diggory, S. (1990). *Schooling: The developing child*. Cambridge, MA: Harvard University Press.

Feller, R., & Walz, G. (Eds.). (1996). *Career transitions in turbulent times: Exploring work, learning, and careers*. Greensboro, NC: ERIC Clearinghouse on Counseling and Student Services (ED 398 519). Retrieved from files.eric.ed.gov/fulltext/ED398519.pdf

Fowler, G. A. (2013, October 8). An early report card on massive open online courses. *Wall Street Journal*. Retrieved from wsj.com/articles/an-early-report-card-on-massive-open-online-courses-1381266504?tesla=y

Frederiksen, N. (1950). *Adjustment to college: A study of 10,000 veteran and non-veteran students in sixteen American colleges*. Princeton, NJ: Educational Testing Service.

Frederiksen, N. (1984). The real test bias. *American Psychologist, 39*(3), 193–202.

Friedman, T. L. (2006). *The world is flat: A brief history of the twenty-first century*. New York: Farrar, Straus, and Giroux.

Fulghum, R. (1989). *All I really need to know I learned in kindergarten: Uncommon thoughts on common things*. New York: Ballantine.

Fullilove, R. E., & Treisman, P. U. (1990). Mathematics achievement among African American undergraduates at the University of California, Berkeley: An evaluation of the mathematics workshop program. *Journal of Negro Education, 59*(3), 463–478.

Gee, J. P. (2003). *What video games have to teach us about learning and literacy*. New York: Palgrave Macmillan.

Gee, J. P. (2013). *The anti-education era*. New York: Palgrave Macmillan.

Gee, J. P., & Hayes, B. (2009). Public pedagogy through video games: Design, resources, & affinity spaces. *Game-based learning*. Retrieved from http://www.gamebasedlearning.org.uk/content/view/59/

Gershenfeld, N. (2012, September). How to make almost anything: The digital fabrication revolution. *Foreign Affairs*. Retrieved from iaac.net/archivos/events/pdf/how-to-make-almost-anything-fo.pdf

Giles, J. (2005, December 15). Internet encyclopedias go head to head. *Nature, 438*, 900–901.

Hagel, J., & Brown, J. S. (2005). *The only sustainable edge: Why business strategy depends on productive friction and dynamic specialization*. Cambridge, MA: Harvard Business School Press.

Halverson, E. R., Lowenhaupt, R., Gibbons, D., & Bass, M. (2009). Conceptualizing identity in youth media arts organizations: A comparative case study. *E-Learning and Digital Media, 6*(1), 23–42.

Halverson, R., Kallio, J., Hackett, S., & Halverson, E. (2016). *Participatory culture as a model for how new media technologies can change public schools* (WCER Working Paper No. 2016-7). Madison, WI: University of Wisconsin Center for Education Research. Retrieved from wcer.wisc.edu/publications/working-papers/

Hamilton, S. F. (1990). *Apprenticeship for adulthood: Preparing youth for the future*. New York: Free Press.

Hanushek, E. A., & Raymond, M. E. (2005). Does school accountability lead to improved student performance? *Journal of Policy Analysis and Management, 24*(2), 297–327.

Hart, P. D. (2006). *Report findings based on a survey among California ninth and tenth graders*. Washington, DC: Peter D. Hart Research Associates. Retrieved from connectedcalifornia.org/downloads/irvine_poll.pdf

Henkoff, R. (1996, January 15). So you want to change your job. *Fortune, 133*(1), 52–56.

Herold, B. (2014, June 9). Technology tools for managing schools face stagnant market. *Education Week, 33*(35), 18.

Herold, B. (2015, June 10). Why ed tech is not transforming how teachers teach. *Education Week*. Retrieved from edweek.org/ew/articles/2015/06/11/why-ed-tech-is-not-transforming-how.html

Ito, M. (2008). Introduction. In K. Varnelis (Ed.), *Networked publics*. Cambridge, MA: MIT Press. Retrieved from itofisher.com/mito/publications/. 1-14.

Ito, M., Baumer, S., Bittanti, M., boyd, d., Cody, R., Herr-Stephenson, B.,..., Tripp, L. (2010). *Hanging out, messing around, and geeking out: Kids living and learning with new media*. Cambridge, MA: MIT Press.

Ito, M., Horst, H., Bittanti, M., Boyd, D., Herr-Stephenson, B., Lange, P. G.,..., Robinson, L. (2008). *Living and learning with new media: Summary of findings from the Digital Youth Project*. Chicago, IL: MacArthur Foundation Digital Media and Learning Project.

Jenkins, H. (2008). *Convergence culture: Where old and new media collide*. New York: NYU Press.

Jenkins, H., Purushotma, R., Clinton, K., Weigel, M., & Robison, A. (2007). *Confronting the challenges of participatory culture: Media education for the 21st century*. Chicago: MacArthur Foundation Digital Media and Learning White Paper Series. Retrieved from newmedialiteracies.org/files/working/NMLWhitePaper.pdf

Johnson, S. B. (2005). *Everything bad is good for you: How today's popular culture is actually making us smarter*. New York: Riverhead Press.

Jones, G., Jones, B., & Hargrove, T. (2003). *The unintended consequences of high-stakes testing*. Lanham, MD: Rowman & Littlefield.

Kamenetz, A. (2010). *DIY U: Edupunks, edupreneurs, and the coming transformation of higher education*. Boston, MA: Chelsea Green.

Knobel, M. (2008, April). *Studying animé music video remix as a new literacy*. Paper presented at the annual meeting of the American Educational Research Association, New York.

Koedinger, K. R., & Anderson, J. R. (1998). Illustrating principled design: The early evolution of a cognitive tutor for algebra symbolization. *Interactive Learning Environments, 5*(2), 161–180.

Kop, R., & Fournier, H. (2010, Fall). New dimensions to self-directed learning in an open networked learning environment. *International Journal of Self-Directed Learning, 7*(2). Retrieved from http://nparc.nrc-cnrc.gc.ca/eng/view/object/?id=c4dc46c9-ef59-46b8-af01-4a7fec44b023

Kozol, J. (2005). *The shame of a nation: The restoration of apartheid schooling in America.* New York: Three Rivers Press.

Lagemann, E. L. (2000). *An elusive science: The troubling history of educational research.* Chicago, IL: University of Chicago Press.

Lang, L., Torgesen, J. K., Vogel, W., Chanter, C., Lefsky, E., & Petscher, Y. (2009). Exploring the relative effectiveness of reading interventions for high school students. *Journal of Research on Educational Effectiveness, 2,* 149–175.

Lanier, J. (2011). *You are not a gadget: A manifesto.* New York: Knopf.

Lave, J. (1988). *The culture of acquisition and the practice of understanding.* Report No. IRL88-0007. Palo Alto, CA: Institute for Research on Learning.

Leander, K., & Boldt, G. (2008, April). *New literacies in old literacy skins.* Paper presented at the annual meeting of the American Educational Research Association, New York.

Lenhart, A. (2015). *Teens, social media, & technology overview 2015.* Pew Research Center on Internet and Technology. Retrieved from pewinternet.org/2015/04/09/teens-social-media-technology-2015/

Lesgold, A., Lajoie, S., Bunzo, M., & Eggan, G. (1992). Sherlock: A coached practice environment for an electronics troubleshooting job. In J. Larkin, R. Chabay, & C. Scheftic (Eds.), *Computer-assisted instruction and intelligent tutoring systems* (pp. 201–255). Hillsdale, NJ: Lawrence Erlbaum Associates.

Levin, R. A., & Hines, L. M. (2003). Educational television, Fred Rogers, and the history of education. *History of Education Quarterly, 43*(2), 262–275.

Lewis, M. (2001). *Next: The future just happened.* New York: W. W. Norton.

Lou, N., & Peck, K. (2016, February 23). By the numbers: The rise of the Makerspace. *Popular Science.* Retrieved from popsci.com/rise-makerspace-by-numbers

Maeroff, G. I. (2003). *A classroom of one: How online learning is changing our schools and colleges.* New York, NY: Palgrave Macmillan.

Means, B., Padilla, C., & Gallagher, L. (2010). *Use of education data at the local level: From accountability to instructional improvement.* U.S. Department of Education Office of Planning, Evaluation, and Policy Development. Retrieved from ed.gov/about/offices/list/opepd/ppss/reports.html#edtech

Metz, M. H. (1990). Real school: A universal drama and disparate experience. In D. E. Mitchell & M. E. Goertz (Eds.), *Education politics for the new century: The twentieth anniversary yearbook of the Politics of Education Association* (pp. 75–92). Philadelphia, PA: Falmer Press.

Mislevy, R., Steinberg, L., Breyer, F., & Almond, R. L. (2002). Making sense of data from complex assessments. *Applied Measurement in Education, 15*(2), 363–389.

Murnane, R. J., & Levy, F. (1996). *Teaching the new basic skills.* New York: Free Press.

National Center for Education Statistics (NCES). (2006). *Homeschooling in the United States: 2003.* Washington, DC: NCES. Retrieved from nces.ed.gov/pubsearch/pubsinfo.asp?pubid=2006042

National Center for Education Statistics (NCES). (2007). *Crime indicators.* Washington, DC: NCES. Retrieved from nces.ed.gov/programs/crimeindicators/crimeindicators2007/

National Center for Education Statistics (NCES). (2015). Table 218.10. Number and Internet access of instructional computers and rooms in public schools, by selected school characteristics: Selected years, 1995 through 2008. Washington, DC: NCES. Retrieved from nces.ed.gov/programs/digest/d15/tables/dt15_218.10.asp?current=yes

Norman, D. A. (1988). *The design of everyday things.* New York: Currency/Doubleday.

Norris, C., & Soloway, E. (2003). The viable alternative: Handhelds. *School Administrator, 60*(4), 26–28.

Olson, D. R. (1994). *The world on paper: The conceptual and cognitive implications of writing and reading.* Cambridge, UK: Cambridge University Press.

Olson, L. (1997). *The school to work revolution: How employers and educators are joining forces to prepare tomorrow's skilled workforce.* New York: Perseus.

Olson, M. (1982). *The rise and decline of nations.* New Haven, CT: Yale University Press.

Ong, W. J. (1982). *Orality and literacy: The technologizing of the word.* London, UK: Routledge.

Orfield, G., & Lee, C. (2007, August 29). *Historic reversals, accelerating resegregation, and the need for new integration strategies.* Los Angeles, CA: UCLA Civil Rights Project/ProyectoDerechos Civiles.

Packer, A. (1997). Mathematical competencies that employers expect. In L. A. Steen (Ed.), *Why numbers count: Quantitative literacy for tomorrow's America* (pp. 137–154). New York, NY: College Entrance Examination Board.

Papert, S. (1980). *Mindstorms: Children, computers, and powerful ideas.* New York: Basic Books.

Patru, M., & Balaji, V. (2016). *Making sense of MOOCs: A guide for policy-makers in developing countries.* Paris, France: UNESCO.

Phillips, D., & Cohen, J. (2013). *Learning gets personal: How Idaho students and teachers are embracing personalized learning through Khan Academy.* Boise, ID: J. A. and Kathryn Albertson Family Foundation.

Postman, N. (1982). *The disappearance of childhood*. New York: Delacorte.

Postman, N. (1985). *Amusing ourselves to death: Public discourse in the age of show business*. New York: Viking Penguin.

Postman, N. (1995, October 9). Virtual students, digital classroom. *The Nation,* 377–382.

Powell, A. G., Farrar, E., & Cohen, D. K. (1985). *The shopping mall high school: Winners and losers in the educational marketplace*. Boston, MA: Houghton Mifflin.

Putnam, R. D. (2000). *Bowling alone: The collapse and revival of American community*. New York: Simon & Schuster.

Rideout, V. J., Foehr, U. G., & Roberts, D. F. (2010). *Generation M2: Media in the lives of 8- to 18-year-olds*. Menlo Park, CA: Kaiser Family Foundation. Retrieved from http://www.kff.org/entmedia/upload/8010.pdf

Rivard, R. (2013, July 18). Udacity project on "pause." *Inside Higher Ed*. Retrieved from insidehighered.com/news/2013/07/18/citing-disappointing-student-outcomes-san-jose-state-pauses-work-udacity

Rodriguez, R. (1982). *Hunger of memory: The education of Richard Rodriguez*. New York: Bantam Books.

Rosenbaum, J. E. (1989, Winter). What if good jobs depended on good grades? *American Educator, 13*(3), 10–15, 40–42.

Rosenbaum, J. E. (2001). *Beyond college for all: Career paths for the forgotten half*. New York: Russell Sage.

Russell, M., & Haney, W. (1997). Testing writing on computers: An experiment comparing student performance on tests conducted via computer and via paper-and-pencil. *Education Policy Analysis Archives, 5*(3). Retrieved from eric.ed.gov/?id=EJ580763

Sadler, P. M. (1987). Misconceptions in astronomy. In J. Novak (Ed.), *Misconceptions and educational strategies in science and mathematics* (pp. 422–437). Ithaca, NY: Cornell University Press.

SCANS Commission. (1991). *What work requires of schools: A SCANS report for America 2000*. Washington, DC: Secretary's Commission on Achieving Necessary Skills, U.S. Department of Labor.

Schank, R. C., Fano, A., Bell, B., & Jona, M. (1994). The design of goal-based scenarios. *Journal of the Learning Sciences, 3*(4), 305–346.

Schön, D. A. (1983). *The reflective practitioner: How professionals think in action*. New York: Basic Books.

Shaffer, D. W. (2004). Pedagogical praxis: The professions as models for post-industrial education. *Teachers College Record, 106*(7), 1401–1421.

Shaffer, D. W. (2006). *How computer games help children learn*. New York: Palgrave.

Shah, D. (2016, December 25). *By the numbers: MOOCS in 2016*. Retrieved from class-central.com/report/mooc-stats-2016/

Shepard, L. (2010). What the marketplace has brought us: Item-by-item teaching with little instructional insight. *Peabody Journal of Education, 85*(2), 246–257.

Sheridan, K., Halverson, E., Litts, B., Brahms, L., Jacobs-Priebe, L., & Owens, T. (2014, Winter). Learning in the making: A comparative case study of three makerspaces. *Harvard Educational Review, 84*(4), 505–531.

Shulman, L. (1986, February). Those who understand: Knowledge growth in teaching. *Educational Researcher*, 4–14.

Singer, N. (2017, May 13). How Google took over the classroom. *New York Times*. Retrieved from nytimes.com/2017/05/13/technology/google-education-chromebooks-schools.html?_r=0

Squire, K. (2006). From content to context: Videogames as designed experience. *Educational Researcher, 35*(1), 19–29.

Squire, K. D. (2004). Sid Meier's *Civilization III. Simulations and Gaming, 35*(1), 135–140.

Stallard, C. H., & Cocker, J. S. (2001). *The promise of technology in schools: The next 20 years*. Lanham, MD: Scarecrow Press.

Steinkuehler, C. (2006). Virtual worlds, learning, & the new pop cosmopolitanism. *Teachers College Record, 12*(84).

Steinkuehler, C. (2008). Massively multiplayer online games as an educational technology: An outline for research. *Educational Technology, 48*(1), 10–21.

Sztajn, P., Confrey, J., Wilson, P. H., & Edgington, C. (2014). Learning trajectory based instruction: Toward a theory of teaching. *Educational Researcher, 41*(5), 147–156.

Tapscott, D. (1988). *Growing up digital: The rise of the Net Generation*. New York: McGraw-Hill.

Thornburg, D. D. (1992). *Edutrends 2010: Restructuring, technology, and the future of education*. San Carlos, CA: Starsong Publications.

Turkle, S. (2015). *Reclaiming conversation: The power of talk in a digital age*. New York: Penguin.

Twenge, J. M. (2017). *iGen: Why today's super-connected kids are growing up less rebellious, more tolerant, less happy—and completely unprepared for adulthood—and what that means for the rest of us*. New York: Atria Books.

Tyack, D., & Cuban, L. (1995). *Tinkering toward utopia: A century of public school reform*. Cambridge, MA: Harvard University Press.

Tyack, D. B. (1974). *The one best system: A history of American urban education*. Cambridge, MA: Harvard University Press.

Tyner, K. (1994). *Access in a digital age*. San Francisco: Strategies for Media Literacy.

Vinovskis, M. A. (1995). *Education, society, and economic opportunity: A historical perspective on persistent issues*. New Haven, CT: Yale University Press.

White, B. Y., & Frederiksen, J. R. (1998). Inquiry, modeling, and metacognition: Making science accessible to all students. *Cognition and Instruction, 16*(1), 3–118.

White, B. Y., & Frederiksen, J. R. (2005). A theoretical framework and approach for fostering metacognitive development. *Educational Psychologist, 40*(4), 211–223.

Williams, C. (2016, January 12). Traditional TV viewing is over: YouTube habit is permanent, warn researchers. *The Telegraph.* Retrieved from telegraph.co.uk/finance/newsbysector/mediatechnologyandtelecoms/media/12067340/Traditional-TV-viewing-is-over-YouTube-habit-is-permanent-warn-researchers.html

Yazzie-Mintz, E. (2006). Voices of students on engagement: A report on the 2006 high school survey of student engagement. Retrieved from ceep.indiana.edu/hssse/pdf/ HSSSE_2006_Report.pdf

Zuboff, S. (1988). *In the age of the smart machine: The future of work and power.* New York: Basic Books.

Index

About the Authors

Allan Collins is Professor Emeritus of Learning Sciences at Northwestern University. He is a member of the National Academy of Education, a fellow of the American Association for Artificial Intelligence, the Cognitive Science Society, the American Association for the Advancement of Science, and the American Educational Research Association. He served as a founding editor of the journal *Cognitive Science* and as first chair of the Cognitive Science Society. He is best known in psychology for his work on semantic memory and mental models, in artificial intelligence for his work on plausible reasoning and intelligent tutoring systems, and in education for his work on inquiry teaching, cognitive apprenticeship, situated learning, design research, epistemic games, and systemic validity in educational testing. From 1991 to 1994 he was co-director of the U.S. Department of Education's Center for Technology in Education. His latest book, *What's Worth Teaching: Rethinking Curriculum in the Age of Technology,* was published by Teachers College Press in April 2017.

Richard Halverson is a professor of Educational Leadership and Policy Analysis in the UW-Madison School of Education. His research aims to bring the research methods and practices of the Learning Sciences to the world of educational leadership and interactive media. Rich co-directs the Wisconsin Collaborative Education Research Network and the Comprehensive Assessment of Leadership for Learning project, and he was a co-founder and co-director the Games + Learning + Society Research Center. A former high school teacher and administrator, he earned an MA in philosophy and a PhD in the learning sciences from Northwestern University. He is co-author (with Carolyn Kelley) of *Mapping Leadership: The Tasks that Matter for Improving Teaching and Learning in Schools.*